Scottish-American Wills,
1650 - 1900

Scottish-American WILLS

1650-1900

David Dobson

CLEARFIELD

Library of Congress Catalogue Card Number 90-86137

Reprinted for Clearfield Company
by Genealogical Publishing Company
Baltimore, Maryland
2010

ISBN 978-0-8063-1296-5

Acknowledgment
The compiler wishes to acknowledge the assistance
of Frances McDonnell in the production of this volume.

Made in the United States of America

Introduction

etween 1650 and 1900 over 2,000 Scots, resident in North America, chose to have their wills registered and confirmed in Scotland rather than in the Prerogative Court of Canterbury, which traditionally had jurisdiction in probate matters affecting British subjects who died overseas. Initially, Scots overseas had their wills confirmed by the Commissariat Court of Edinburgh, though later this became a function of the Sheriff Court of Edinburgh. The records of both courts are now housed in the Scottish Record Office, Edinburgh.

This book is essentially an index to all such wills, or, more accurately, an index to the testaments and inventories of those Scots-Americans who died and had their wills confirmed in Scotland prior to 1900, with supplementary data extracted from a government publication entitled *Index to Personal Estates of Defuncts, 1846-1866* (Edinburgh, 1866). Should it be desired, further information can be obtained from the Scottish Record Office by citing the document reference number given at the end of each entry.

David Dobson

N.B. As used in the text, "ex" means "from."

Scottish-American Wills,
1650-1900

Abstahs, Caroline, in New York, reg. 1896.   (SC.1.363)

Adam, Patrick, ex Arbroath, in Kingston, Jamaica, reg. 16 June
    1761.   (CC8.8.118)

Adam, William, ex Aberdeen, d. 1698 in Darien, reg. 1707.
    (CC8.8.83)

Affleck, Robert, physician in Kingston, Grenada, reg. 1867.
    (SC70.1.133)

Agnew, George, overseer, d. 1699 in Darien, reg. 1707.
    (CC8.8.84)

Agnew, Thomas, ex Wigtownshire, d. 4 Sept. 1843 in USA,
    reg. 1866.   (SC70.1.66)(F196)

Aiken, Alexander, ex Bo'ness, sailor, d. 1699 in Darien,
    reg. 1707.   (CC8.8.83)

Aitchison, Peter, physician & surgeon in St Elizabeth's,
    Jamaica, d. 1752, reg. 3 Apr. 1758.   (CC8.8.117)

Aitken, George, in St Croix, d. 26 Jan. 1815, reg. 1829.
    (D7)

Aitken, James, ex Islay, clergyman in America, reg. 1 Sept.
    1783.   (CC8.8.126)

Aitkenhead, William, in St Thomas in the Vale, Jamaica,
    reg. 30 June 1768.   (CC8.8.121)

Airston, William Glen, in Sarawak, Grey Co, Canada, reg. 1890.
    (SC70.1.287)

Alexander, Charles, in Montreal, St Patrick's, Grenada,
    d. 5 Oct. 1861 in London, reg. 1862.   (SC70.1.111)

Alexander, George, in Durham, Drummond Co, Lower Canada,
    reg. 1856.   (SC70.1.89)

Alexander, George, in Halifax, Nova Scotia, reg. 1872.
    (SC70.1.156)

1

Alexander, Isabella, in Grenada, reg. 1869.   (SC70.1.145)

Alexander, John, merchant in Carolina, d. 8 Oct. 1699,
     reg. 29 Jan. 1707.   (CC8.8.83)

Alexander, Mary, in St Lucia, d. 10 Feb. 1818, reg. 6 Jan.
     1819.   (CC8.8.145)

Alexander, Robert, in Jackson, New York, reg. 1866.
     (SC70.1.128)

Allan, Ann, in Brant, Ontario, reg. 1877.   (SC70.1.186)

Allan, Arthur Edward, shipowner in Montreal, reg. 1894.
     (SC70.1.326)

Allan, Colin, surgeon in Frederickton, New Brunswick,
     d. 16 July 1850, reg. 1852.   (SC70.1.73)(E2790)

Allan, Hugh, in Ravenscraig, Montreal, reg. 1886.   (SC70.1.246)

Allan, James, ex Tranent, carter in Canada, reg. 1853.
     (SC70.1.65)

Allan, William Spence, in Beverley, Canada, d. 28 Feb. 1843,
     reg. 1847.   (SC70.1.68)(F611)

Allen, David, ex Musselburgh, seaman, d. 1699 in Darien,
     reg. 1707.   (CC8.8.83)

Allison, Agnes, in Mifflintown, Pennsylvania, d. 19 Feb.
     1863, reg. 1865.   (SC70.1.123)(G3735)

Alston, David, in Kingston, St Vincent, reg. 1831.   (SC70.1.43)

Amezaga, Jose Manuel, in Mexico, reg. 1883.   (SC70.1.222)

Amos, William, in Egremont, Canada, reg. 1866.   (SC70.1.129)

Anderson, Alexander, sailor, d. 1699 in Darien, reg. 1707.
     (CC8.8.83)

Anderson, George, ex St Andrews, clergyman, d. 1698 in
     Darien, reg. 1707.   (CC8.8.83)

2

Anderson, Alexander, in Salaberry, Valleyfield, Canada,
    reg. 1882. (SC70.1.213)

Anderson, Andrew, merchant in Grenada & Antigua, reg. 26 May
    1784. (CC8.8.126)

Anderson, Archibald Thomas, in Toronto, reg. 1898.
    (SC70.1.372)

Anderson, Charles, in Jamaica, d. Jan. 1815, reg. 27 Oct.
    1815. (CC8.8.141)(SC70.1.14)

Anderson, Charles, in Riverhead, Jamaica, d. 19 May 1853 in
    Edinburgh, reg. 1853. (SC70.1.53)(E3489)

Anderson, David, brassfinisher in Toronto, reg. 1891.
    (SC70.1.298)

Anderson, Ebenezer, ex Cupar, Fife, farmer in Detroit, reg.
    1892. (SC70.1.307)

Anderson, Edgar, in Schuyler, Illinois, reg. 1882.
    (SC70.1.216)

Anderson, James, ex Elgin, housewright in Jamaica, d. Mar. 1775,
    reg. 8 Nov. 1776. (CC8.8.123)

Anderson, James, ex Leith, merchant in Brooksbank, Essex Co,
    Virginia, d. 3 Mar. 1788, reg. 17 Sep. 1788.
    (CC8.8.127)

Anderson, James, carpenter in Jamaica, d. Dec. 1830,
    reg. 1832. (SC70.1.46)(D359)

Anderson, John David, civil engineer in Bermuda, d. 31 July
    1857, reg. 1858. (SC70.1.96)(H401)

Anderson, John Henderson, draper's assistant in Rhode Island,
    reg. 1882. (SC70.1.218)

Anderson, Margaret, in Brooklyn, reg. 1882. (SC70.1.215)

Anderson, Mary, in Canada, reg. 1871. (SC70.1.155)

Anderson, Porter, in Schuyler, Illinois, reg. 1882.
    (SC70.1.218)

Anderson, Robert, in Sydney, Nova Scotia, reg. 1871.
    (SC70.1.151)   3

Anderson, William, ex Edinburgh, shoemaker, d. 1698 in
    Darien, reg. 1707. (CC8.8.83)

Anderson, William, ex Arbroath, sailor, d. 1698 in
    Darien, reg. 1707. (CC8.8.83)

Anderson, William, ex Fife, mariner, d. 1698 in Darien,
    reg. 1707. (CC8.8.83)

Anderson, William, ex Leith, brewer, d. 1698 in Darien,
    reg. 1707. (CC8.8.83)

Andrew, Alexander, millwright in Trinidad, d. Jan. 1840,
    reg. 1846. (SC70.1.67)(F354)

Andrew, James, ex Edinburgh, sailor, d. 1698 in Darien,
    reg. 1707. (CC8.8.83)

Angus, Gilbert, ex Burntisland, sailor, d. 1698 in Darien,
    reg. 1707. (CC8.8.83)

Angus, John, mariner, d. 1698 in Darien, reg. 1707.
    (CC8.8.83)

Angus, Robert, engineer in the West Indies, reg. 1859.
    (SC70.1.107)

Angus, Thomas McQuiston, in Jamaica, d. 25 Aug. 1825, reg. 1831.
    (SC70.1.44)(C349)

Annan, Robert, clergyman in York Co, Pennsylvania, reg.
    1891. (SC70.1.292)

Annell, Magnus, ex Orkney, d. 1790 at Hudson Bay, reg. 1 July
    1795. (CC8.8.30)

Aquart, Jean Marie, in St Lucia, d. 29 May 1838, reg. 1841.
    (SC70.1.60)(D1463)

Arbuthnott, Thomas, ex Peterhead, surgeon in Virginia,
    d. 10 Nov. 1742, reg. 6 Feb. 1745. (CC8.8.109)

Archibald, Jessie, da of George Archibald in St Vincent,
    d. 29 May 1830 in Edinburgh, reg. 1831.
    (SC70.1.43)(C371)

Archibald, John, ex Burntisland, sailor, d. 1698 in Darien,
    reg. 1707. (CC8.8.83)

4

Archibald, John, in Darien, USA, reg. 1883. (SC70.1.226)

Arthur, Mary, in Boston, reg. 1887. (SC70.1.257)

Arthur, William, in Brooklyn, New York, reg. 1876.
   (SC70.1.179)

Aris, Douglas, ex Liverpool, d. Apr. 1825 at Montego Bay,
   Jamaica, reg. 18 Apr. 1827. (CC8.8.151)(SC70.1.36)

Armour, Robert, physician in Trinidad, d. 19 Apr. 1840,
   reg. 1842. (SC70.1.61)(C2779)

Armour, William, engineer in Jamaica, reg. 1894. (SC70.1.326)

Arthur, Mary, ex Ascog, Bute, d. 2 Feb. 1853 in Jamaica, reg.
   1857. (SC70.1.93)(G407)

Ash, John Hill, in St Mary's, Perth, Canada, reg. 1884.
   (SC70.1.350)

Aspinwall, Anna Ross, in Pittsburgh, reg. 1895. (SC70.1.350)

Athill, John, in Antigua, d. 6 Aug. 1842, reg. 1842.
   (SC70.1.63)(C2976)

Auchterlonie, James Scott, in Toronto, reg. 1893.
   (SC70.1.321)

Auld, John, ex Glasgow, merchant in Virginia, reg. 28 Oct.
   1803. (CC8.8.134)

Auld, Robert, in Tobago, d. 16 June 1862, reg. 1865.
   (SC70.1.120)(H1647)

Baillie, John, ex Peebles-shire, surgeon, d. 1699 in Darien,
    reg. 1707. (CC8.8.83)

Baillie, William, soldier, d. 1699 in Darien, reg. 1707
    (CC8.8.83)

Bain, Archibald, ex Glasgow, baker, d. 1812 in St John's,
    Antigua, reg. 1853. (SC70.1.78)(F1596)

Bain, James, in New York, d. Jul. 1848, reg. 1853. (SC70.1.79)
    (E3467)

Bain, William, ex Fife, sailor, d. 1699 in Darien, reg. 1707.
    (CC8.8.83)

Baird, John, in Brownsville, Lee Co, Oklahoma, reg. 1889.
    (SC70.1.276)

Baird, Peter, mariner, in Virginia, d. 21 Nov. 1880, reg.
    28 Mar. 1812. (CC8.8.138)

Bainbridge, Mary, in USA, reg. 1898. (SC70.1.348)

Bairnsfather, William, baker in Jamaica, d. 1791, reg.
    20 Feb. 1794. (CC8.8.129)

Balfour, John, merchant in Black River, Jamaica, reg.
    9 Nov. 1750. (CC8.8.113)

Balfour, John, merchant planter in Peedee River, South
    Carolina, d. 15 Nov. 1781, reg 26 Jun. 1783.
    (CC8.8.126)

Balfour, William, ex Fife, mariner, d. 1698 in Darien,
    reg. 1707. (CC8.8.83)

Ball, Ingram, in Oak Farm, Cape Breton, d. 18 Mar. 1807,
    reg. 28 Dec. 1821. (CC8.8.147)

Ball, Ingram, in Oak Farm, Cape Breton, Nova Scotia, reg.
    1888. (SC70.1.263)

Ballantyne, John, ex Leith, seaman, d. 1698 in Darien,
    reg. 1707. (CC8.8.83)

Ballentyne, George, sailor, d. 1699 in Darien, reg. 1707.
    (CC8.8.84)

Balloch, Janet, in Ontario, reg. 1875.   (SC70.1.173)

Ballon, Angello, sailor, d. 1698 in Darien, reg. 1707.
   (CC8.8.83)

Ballingal, Thomas, in Waterloo, Ontario, reg. 1888.
   (SC70.1.267)

Balloch, John, book-keeper in Jamaica, d. 1835, reg. 1844.
   (SC70.1.66)(F118)

Balmer, Robert, merchant in Montreal, d. 20 Feb. 1860, reg.
   1860.   (SC70.1.106)(G1946)

Balnaves, Robert, steward, d. 1698 in Darien, reg. 1707.
   (CC8.8.83)

Bannatyne, William, ex Edinburgh, sailor, d. 1698 in Darien,
   reg. 1707.   (CC8.8.84)

Baptie, John, steward, d. 1698 in Darien, reg. 1707.
   (CC8.8.83)

Baptista, Joannes, sailor, d. 1698 in Darien, reg. 1707.
   (CC8.8.83)

Barclay, Hugh, stewart, d. 1699 in Darien, reg. 1707.
   (CC8.8.83)

Barclay, John, in Carriacou, Grenada, d. 1801 in Cupar, Fife,
   reg. 1801.   (SC20.33.14)

Barclay, Peter, in Hazlegreen, Wisconsin, reg. 1876.
   (SC70.1.178)

Barclay, William, ex Edinburgh, sailor, d. 1699 in Darien,
   reg. 1707.   (CC8.8.83)

Barr, Elizabeth, in Canada, reg. 1844.   (SC70.1.66)

Barr, Thomas, miner in Terre Haute, Indiana, reg. 1884.
   (SC70.1.234)

Bartram, Christian, ex Burntisland, sailor, d. 1698 in Darien,
   reg. 1707.   (CC8.8.83)

Baxter, John, in Grenada, reg. 1822.   (SC70.1.27)

Bayley, Thomas Elder, merchant in Franklin, USA, reg. 1875.
    (SC70.1.174)

Bayne, Penelope Sober, in 29 E 29th St, New York, reg. 1884.
    (SC70.1.231)

Beatson, James, in Canada West, reg. 1856.   (SC70.1.90)

Beck, William J, in Morrisiania, USA, reg. 1878.   (SC70.1.190)

Belfou, Pierre Aman, in Carricou, Grenada, d. 4 Aug. 1842,
    reg. 1843.   (SC70.1.63)(C3028)

Bell, George, ex London, merchant, d. 20 Oct. 1841 in Acoyaba,
    Central America, reg. 1849.   (SC70.1.69)(F889)

Bell, John, ex Glasgow, in Jamaica, reg. 30 Dec. 1773.
    (CC8.8.122)

Bell, John, in St Mary's, Jamaica, d. 8 Sep. 1843, reg. 1844.
    (SC70.1.65)(E75)

Bell, John, merchant in St Louis, Missouri, d. 30 Mar. 1860,
    reg. 1861.   (SC70.1.108)(H1006)

Bell, Richard, s of Richard Bell, ex Tanlawhill, Dumfries-shire,
    in New York, d. Jun. 1857, reg. 1860.   (SC70.1.103)
    (H765)

Bennet, Fullarton, in Lillington, USA, reg. 1877.   (SC70.1.186)

Bennet, William, steward, d. 9 Aug. 1862 in Key West, USA,
    reg. 1863.   (SC70.1.118)(H1427)

Bennett, Henry, ex Fife, carpenter, d. 1698 in North America,
    reg. 1707.   (CC8.8.83)

Bernier, Ferdinand, in Haiti, reg. 1898.   (SC70.1.370)

Berrie, James, conveyancer in Ingersoll, Canada West,
    d. 23 Apr. 1864, reg 1864.   (SC70.1.122)(H1739)

8

Berry, Francis, ex Leith, mariner, d. 1698 in Darien, reg. 1707
   (CC8.8.83)

Berry, James, ex Jamaica, merchant, d. Glasgow, reg. 22 Aug. 1817.
   (CC9.9.83)

Bethune, Robert, in Thorah, Ontario, d. 15 Jan. 1864, reg. 1864.
   (SC70.1.121)(G3523)

Bethune, Robert Henry, banker in Toronto, reg. 1897.   (SC70.1355)

Bethune, Unagh, in Thorah, Ontario, reg. 1886.   (SC70.1.247)

Betts, Henry Augustus, in Portsmouth, Ontario, reg. 1877.
   (SC70.1.186)

Bewly, John Pearson, in Branchville, USA, reg. 1881.
   (SC70.1.211)

Bews, William, in Hamilton, Canada, reg. 1900.   (SC70.1.393)

Biggar, George, in New Jersey, reg. 1899.   (SC70.1.377)

Birch, John Forbes, in Mexico, reg. 1884.   (SC70.1.232)

Birrell, James, ex Fife, sailor, d. 1698 in Darien, reg. 1707.
   (CC8.8.83)

Birrell, Margaret, in Pickering, Ontario, reg. 1896.
   (SC70.1.346)

Black, Angus, in Winnipeg, reg. 1883.   (SC70.1.221)

Black, Henry, sailor, d. 1698 in Darien, reg. 1707.
   (CC8.8.83)

Black, James, ex Edinburgh, sailor, d. 1698 in Darien, reg. 1707.
   (SC70.1.83)

Black, John, in Falmouth, Jamaica, reg. 1826.   (SC70.1.35)

Black, Joseph, soldier, Voluntary Artillery, in New York,
   d. 21 Jul. 1847, reg. 1857.   (SC70.1.94)(H291)

9

Black, Mary, in Long Beach, California, reg. 1899.
(SC70.1.380)

Blackburn, Hugh, in Maryland, d. 5 Jan. 1833, reg. 1836.
(SC70.1.53)(D879)

Blackburn, Mary, in Murraybay, Canada, d. 14 May 1821.   (D3)

Blackie, Burridge, purser in Cuba, reg. 1865.   (SC70.1.124)

Blackie, David, ex Grangepans, sailor, d. 1698 in Darien,
reg. 1707.   (CC8.8.83)

Blackstock, Thomas, in Virginia, reg. 1822.   (SC70.1.26)

Blaikie, William, in Hamilton, Canada, reg. 1859.
(SC70.1.99)

Blair, Ann, ex Perth, in South Carolina, reg. 8 Dec. 1797.
(CC8.8.130)

Blair, Homer, planter in Jamaica, d. Feb. 1832, reg. 1854.
(SC70.1.85)(E4037)

Blair, Joh, ex Perthshire, in Jamaica, d. Jul. 1736, reg.
27 Jun. 1738.   (CC8.8.101)

Blount, Samuel, planter in St Thomas in the East, Jamaica,
d. 1 Oct. 1828, reg. 1833.   (SC70.1.49)(C960)

Blowers, Archibald, in Nova Scotia, reg. 1895.   (SC70.1.337)

Blyth, David, cooper in Montreal, d. Jan. 1829, reg. 1833.
(SC70.1.48)(D459)

Blyth, John, in Kendall, Jamaica, d. 1 Jun. 1835, reg. 1838.
(SC70.1.56)(C1908)

Boag, Robert, in Jamiaca, d. Edinburgh, reg. 1813.
(SC70.1.8)

Boigs, John, ex Renfrewshire, sailor, d. 1699 in Darien, reg.
1707.   (CC8.8.83)

Bone, William, spirit-dealer in Chicago, reg. 1870.
    (SC70.1.147)

Boon, Joseph Henry, physician in Basse Terre, St Kitts,
    reg. 1880.   (SC70.1.201)

Bonthron, James, ex Kinghorn, marine, d. 1698 in Darien.
    reg. 1707.   (CC8.8.83)

Boreland, John, storekeeper in Jamaica, d. Sep 1728, reg.
    13 May 1789.   (CC8.8.128)

Borland, Mary Hamilton, in Upper Canada, d. Jan. 1820, reg.
    20 Oct. 1821.   (CC8.8.147)

Boss, Andrew, in La Prairie, Wisconsin, reg. 1868.
    (SC70.1.139)

Bower, John, merchant in Dundee, d. 1699 in Darien, reg. 1707.
    (CC8.8.84)

Bowie, John, ex Newcastle, sailor, d. 1698 in Darien, reg.
    1707.   (CC8.8.83)

Bowman, Archibald, merchant in New York, d. May 1790 in
    Glasgow, reg. 3 Nov. 1790.   (CC9.7.74)

Bowman, Jane McMath, in Lowell, USA, reg. 1895.   (SC70.1.337)

Bowman, Sarah, ex Edinburgh, in Staten Island, New York, reg.
    1889.   (SC70.1.273)

Bowrin, Grace Eliza, in Paradise, Nevis, reg. 1884.
    (SC70.1.229)

Bowrin, Louisa, in Ottawa, reg. 1891.   (SC70.1.296)

Box, Thomas, in Buffalo, USA, reg. 1862.   (SC70.1.212)

Boyd, Ann, w of Alexander Brown, surgeon, in Tobago, d.
    Glasgow, reg. 26 Jan. 1749.   (CC9.7.60)

Boyd, John, clergyman in Freehold, New Jersey, reg. 10 Apr. 1710.
    (CC8.8.84)

Boyd, Robert, merchant in Virginia, reg. 22 Oct. 1783.
    (CC8.8.126)   11

Boyd, Robert, in Reynoldsburg, Franklin County, Ohio, reg. 1890. (SC70.1.289)

Boyd, Thomas, in 278 W 31st St, New York, d. 27 May 1860, reg. 1865. (SC70.1.124)(G3769)

Brander, John, planter in St John's, Grenada, d. May 1806 in Tortula, reg. 16 Jun. 1807. (CC8.8.137)

Brander, John, in Vernon, Pennsylvania, d. 14 Oct. 1863, reg. 1865. (SC70.1.128)(H2019)

Breedon, Benjamin F, merchant in New York, reg. 1874. (SC70.1.168)

Bremner, Alexander, in Bent County, Colorado, reg. 1887. (SC70.1.258)

Briggs, Robert, in Antigua, d. 3 May 1841, reg. 1841. (SC70.1.61)(C2731)

Briggs, Thomas, in Kingston, Frontenac County, Ontario, reg. 1900. (SC70.1.395)

Brock, Andrew, ex Glasgow, gunner, d. 1698 in Darien. reg. 1707. (SC8.8.83)

Brodie, James Arthur, in Colorado, reg. 1891. (SC70.1.298)

Brodie, Elizabeth, in New York, d. 13 Oct. 1857 in Edinburgh, reg. 1859. (SC70.1.101)(G1454)

Brodie, Francis, ex Morayshire, sailor, d. 1698 in Darien, reg. 1707. (CC8.8.83)

Brodie, William, in Tacarigua, Trinidad, reg. 1883. (SC70.1.228)

Broughton, Edward in Quebec, d. 16 Jul. 1854, reg. 1857. (SC70.1.95)(H326)

Brown, Alexander, receiver general in Jamaica, d. 10 Oct. 1770, reg. 17 Dec. 1779. (CC8.8.124)

Brown, Alexander Ogilvy, clergyman in Campbelltown, New Brunswick, reg. 1889. (SC70.1.276)

Brown, Andrew, ex Aberdeen, sailor, d. 1698 in Darien, reg. 1707. (CC8.8.84)

Brown, David, in Somerset County, Maryland, d. 1697. (RH1.2.488)

Brown, David, in North America, reg. 1814. (SC70.1.9)

Brown, David, in St John, New Brunswick, d.1812. reg. 4 Feb. 1814. (CC8.8.140)

Brown, David, ex Glasgow, in Jamaica, d. Aug. 1822, reg. 1835. (SC70.1.52)

Brown, David, in California, reg. 1882. (SC70.1.215)

Brown, Francis, physician in St Vincent, d. 8 Sep. 1829, reg. 1835. (SC70.1.52)(C1237)

Brown, George, in Buffalo, USA, d. 25 Jan. 1863, reg. 1864. (SC70.1.123)(H1795)

Brown, George Allan, clerk in St John, Antigua, d. 27 May 1861 reg. 1863. (SC70.1.116)(H1438)

Brown, James, clerk in Farmington, Georgia, d. 3 Apr. 1851, reg. 1856. (SC70.1.92)(G350)

Brown, James Forrester, clerk in Chicago, reg. 1888. (SC70.1.265)

Brown, John, physician in Williamsburg, Virginia, d. 1727, reg. 20 Aug. 1730. (CC8.8.93)

Brown, John, merchant in Halifax, Nova Scotia, d. 4 May 1834, reg. 1836. (SC70.1.53)(C1430)

Brown, Margaret Craig, in Brandon, Manitoba, reg. 1900. (SC70.1.394)

Brown, Rachel, in Mearville, Pennsylvania, reg. 1877. (SC70.1.182)

Brown, Margaret, in Belleville, Canada, d. 13 Jan. 1844, reg. 1846. (SC70.1.66)(F310)

Brown, Robert, in Low Layton, Jamaica, d. 1837.   (C2322)

Brown, Robert, physician in Richmond, Virginia, reg. 1785.
    (CC5.21.5)

Brown, Sarah, da of James Brown, merchant, in Virginia,
    d. 9 Jun. 1841 in Edinburgh.   (D1484)

Brown, William, sailor, d. 1698 in Darien, reg. 1707.
    (CC8.8.83)

Brown William, in Montreal, reg. 1890.   (SC70.1.282)

Brown, William, in Owen Sound, Ontario, reg. 1897.
    (SC70.1.362)

Browne, Josias Fairly, ex St Vincent, missionary, d. 22 Dec.
    1857 in Cheshire, reg. 1858.   (SC70.1.97)(G919)

Brownlie, Elizabeth, in Osgoode, Carleton, Canada, reg. 1895.
    (SC70.1.337)

Bruce, Thomas, ex Barbados, Captain, 21st Fusiliers, d. 28 Jul.
    1863 in St Thomas, reg. 1864.   (SC70.1.121)(H1652)

Bruce, Thomas Purves, in Oakland, Mississippi, reg. 1896.
    (SC70.1.353)

Bruce, Walter Hamilton, in Montreal, reg. 1875.   (SC70.1.175)

Bruce, William, ex Peterhead, sailor, d. Jul. 1700 in Darien,
    reg. 1707.   (CC8.8.83)

Brunner, William, ex Glasgow, in New York. reg. 1894.
    (SC70.1.336)

Brunton, Margaret, wid of Rev William Brunton, in Argenteuil,
    Canada, d. 25 Oct. 1841, reg. 1843.   (SC70.1.63)

Bryce, Andrew Carter, in Fargo, Dakota, reg. 1887.
    (SC70.1.256)

Bryce, Jessie, in New Orleans, reg. 1892.   (SC70.1.310)

Bryce, Thomas, in Sangamon County, Illinois, reg. 1886.
    (SC70.1.247)

Brydon, Jane, in Quebec, d. 20 Mar. 1829.   (C336)

Brymer, Charles, painter in St Vincent, d. 18 Dec. 1858,
    reg. 1859.   (SC70.1.101)(H653)

Buchan, Charles, d. Flamborough East, Canada West, d. 8 Aug.
    1853, reg. 1854.   (SC70.1.83)(E3794)

Buchan, John Gentles, linen agent in New York, reg. 1884.
    (SC70.1.236)

Buchanan, Agnes, Evelyn, in Niagara, Lincoln, Canada, reg.
    1884.   (SC70.1.241)

Buchanan, Archibald, in Farmington, USA, reg. 1866.
    (SC70.1.131)

Buchanan, Isaac, in Hamilton, Wentworth, Ontario, reg. 1866.
    (SC70.1.254)

Buchanan, Jean, in Newport, St Mary's, Jamaica, d. Glasgow,
    reg. 13 Dec. 1823.   (CC9.7.81)

Buchanan, John, storekeeper in Lowell, Massachusetts, d. Jul. 1859,
    reg. 1865.   (SC70.1.126)(H1932)

Buchanan, John, in Lowell, Massachusetts, d. Jul. 1859, reg.
    1878.   (SC70.1.189)

Buchanan, Mary Louisa, in Brantford, Canada, reg. 1882.
    (SC70.1.219)

Buchanan, Peter, merchant in Charleston, South Carolina, d.
    10 Sep. 1819, reg. 6 Nov. 1820.   (CC8.8.149)(SC70.1.23)

Buchanan, William, surgeon in Bermuda, d. 28 Jun. 1839, reg.
    1839.   (SC70.1.58)(D1278)

Buist, Andrew, in New York, reg. 1891.   (SC70.1.295)

Burgess, John, in New Jersey, reg. 1878.   (SC70.1.187)

Burn, George, in St Vincent, reg. 17 Apr. 1789.   (CC8.8.135)

Burn, John, in St Vincent, reg. 27 Jun. 1805.   (CC8.8.135)

Burn, William, in St Vincent, reg. 17 Apr. 1789.   (CC8.8.128)

Burnet, Robert, ex Unst, Shetland, lighthousekeeper in Chicago,
    reg. 1900.   (SC70.1.389)

Burnett, Henrietta, wid of John Stuart merchant, ex Carolina,
    d. Jan. 1718 in Edinburgh, reg. 1 May 1718.   (CC8.8.87)

Burnett, William, merchant in New York, reg. 1857.   (SC70.1.94)

Burns, David, in San Fernando, Trinidad, reg. 1889.
    (SC709.1.276)

Burt, Patrick, ex Perth, in St Michael's, South Carolina, reg.
    18 Aug. 1775.   (CC8.8.123)

Burton, Robert, in Richmond, Virginia, d. 16 May 1837, reg.
    1839.   (SC70.1.58)(C2128)

Calderwood, George, quartermaster, d. 1698 in Darien, reg. 1707. (CC8.8.83)

Caldwell, John, ex Fife, sailor, d. 1698 in Darien, reg. 1707. (CC8.8.83)

Caldwell, Robert, sailor, d. 1699 in Darien, reg. 1707. (CC8.8.83)

Callendar, John, medical student in Toronto, d. 11 Mar. 1853, reg. 1855. (SC70.1.66)(F1994)

Callum, Thomas, accountant in Quebec, d. 12 Dec. 1846, reg. 1847. (SC70.1.67)(F489)

Camby, Jacob, sailor, d. 1698 in Darien, reg. 1707. (CC8.8.83)

Cameron, Alexander, in Brooklyn, New York, reg. 1884. (SC70.1.231)

Cameron, Margaret, in Peterborough, Ontario, reg. 1884. (SC70.1.233)

Campbell, Angus, in Port of Spain, Trinidad, reg. 1870. (SC70.1.150)

Campbell, Alexander, physician in Jamaica, d. 1751, reg. 17 Nov. 1753. (CC8.8.114)

Campbell, Angus William, in New York, reg. 1893. (SC70.1.315)

Campbell, Charles, physician in Kingston, Jamaica, reg. 1873. (SC70.1.164)

Campbell, Colin, ex Perthshire, soldier, d. 1699 in Jamaica, reg. 1707. (CC8.8.83)

Campbell, Colin, mate, d. 1698 in Darien, reg. 1707. (CC8.8.83)

Campbell, Daniel, ex Airdrie, d. 23 July 1850 in Lake Erie, America. (SC70.1.112)(H1259)

Campbell, Daniel, in Dundee, Kane Co, Illinois, d. 28 Aug. 1860, reg. 1862. (SC70.1.112)(H1259)

Campbell, Duncan, soldier, d. 1699 in Darien, reg. 1707.
(CC8.8.83)

Campbell, Helen, in Milwaukee, Wisconsin, d. 30 July
1850, reg. 1862. (SC70.1.112)(H1258)

Campbell, James, sailor, d. 1699 in Darien, reg. 1707.
(CC8.8.83)

Campbell, James, in Tobago, d. Oct. 1805, reg. Dec. 1809.
(CC8.8.137)

Campbell, James, in Grenada, d. Teignmouth, reg. 1810.
(SC70.1.3)

Campbell, James Hay, in Barrie, Ontario, reg. 1884.
(SC70.1.234)

Campbell, Janet, ex Argyll, in Kingston, Jamaica, d. 1790,
reg. 30 July 1799. (CC8.8.131)

Campbell, John, merchant in Trinidad, d. 24 Aug. 1817,
reg. 25 June 1818. (CC8.8.143)(SC70.1.19)

Campbell, John, ex Glasgow, merchant in Montreal, d. Jan.
1823, reg. 26 Dec. 1823. (CC8.8.149)

Campbell, Maria, ex Glasgow, in Jamaica, d. Glasgow, reg.
11 Dec. 1804. (CC9.7.79)

Campbell, Mary Ann, in Fonda, Montgomery Co, New York, reg.
1885. (SC70.1.247)

Campbell, Patrick, physician in Jamaica, d. Edinburgh,
reg. 2 Mar. 1787. (CC8.8.127)

Campbell, Peter, in St Louis, Missouri, reg. 1878.
(SC70.1.187)

Campbell, William, soldier, d. 1699 in Darien, reg. 1708.
(CC8.8.84)

Campbell, William, ex Argyll, mariner, d. 1699 in Darien,
reg. 1708. (CC8.8.84)

Campbell, William, in Hanover, Jamaica, reg. 12 Nov. 1794.
    (CC8.8.129)

Campbell, William Mark, in 2nd West Indian Regiment,
    d. 25 Oct. 1847 in Nassau, reg. 1852.   (SC70.1.77)(F1542)

Cannon, Eliza M, in New York, reg. 1881.   (SC70.1.204)

Cargill, Louisa, in Boston, reg. 1893.   (SC70.1.326)

Carmichael, Alexander, surgeon in St Croix, d. 5 Jan. 1782,
    reg. 21 Sept. 1782.   (CC8.8.125)

Carmichael, Euphemia Douglas, in New York, reg. 1899.
    (SC70.1.377)

Carmichael, William, cook, d. 1698 in Darien, reg. 1707.
    (CC8.8.83)

Carnegie, John, ex Edinburgh, yeoman, d. 22 Oct. 1699 in
    Darien, reg. 1707.   (CC8.8.83)

Carnegy, John, ex Edinburgh, cook, d. 1698 in Darien,
    reg. 1707.   (CC8.8.83)

Carruth, Andrew, planter in Tobago, reg. 1845.   (SC70.1.66)

Carruthers, James, merchant in Savanna, reg. 1822.
    (SC70.1.26)

Carstairs, James, in Mitford, Canada, reg. 1893.
    (SC70.1.322)

Carsewell, Thomas W, in Guelph, Ontario,reg. 1878.
    (SC70.1.187)

Cassels, Richard Scougall, in Toronto, reg. 1897.
    (SC70.1.355)

Cassills, John, ex Bo'ness, mariner, d. 1698 in Darien,
    reg. 1707.   (CC8.8.83)

Cathcart, Allan, soldier, d. 1699 in Darien, reg. 1707.
    (CC8.8.83)

Cavie, Agnes, in Ontario, reg. 1879.   (SC70.1.197)

Chalmers, David, ex Paisley, weaver in North America,
    reg. 15 Oct. 1787.   (CC8.8.127)

Chalmers, Hector, in Port Antonio, Jamaica, reg. Oct. 1831.
    (D388)

Chalmers, James, ex Paisley, weaver in North America,
    reg. 15 Oct. 1787.   (CC8.8.127)

Chalmers, James, in San Bernardino, California, reg. 1882.
    (SC70.1.211)

Chalmers, James, carpenter at 1014, 10th Ave, New York,
    reg. 1887.   (SC70.1.259)

Chalmers, William, in Dominica, d. 5 July 1811, reg. 1829.
    (SC70.1.41)(D70)

Chambers, John, in St Elizabeth, Jamaica, d. 9 Dec. 1831,
    reg. 1833.   (SC70.1.33)(C929)

Chandler, Jane, in Canada, reg. 1864.   (SC70.1.121)

Chaplin, George, merchant in Kingston, Jamaica, d. May 1723,
    reg. 28 May 1724.   (CC8.8.89)

Chapman, John, in Grenada, reg. 1826.   (SC70.1.34)

Charnock, John, in Manchester, Jamaica, reg. 1850.
    (SC70.1.70)

Charters, George, ex Edinburgh, in Falmouth, Jamaica, d. Dec.
    1841, reg. 1844.   (SC70.1.65)(F28)

Chase, William, in Brookline, Norfolk Co, Massachusetts,
    reg. 1896.   (SC70.1.351)

Christie, Duncan, in Acken, South Carolina, reg. 1882.
    (SC70.1.218)

Christie, Francis Carnegie, merchant in Belize, d. 10 Aug. 1854, reg. 1855. (SC70.1.86)(E4179)

Christie, Peter, in York, Upper Canada, d. 5 Mar. 1827, (B1334)

Christie, Robert Stuart, merchant in Canada, reg. 1892. (SC70.1.308)

Christison, Ann Hay, in Colorado, reg. 1892. (SC70.1.306)

Clark, Alexander, in New Jersey, reg. 1877. (SC70.1.184)

Clark, George, in Hanover, Jamaic, reg. 1781. (CC8.8.125)

Clark, Janet, in Ontario, reg. 1874. (SC70.1.166)

Clark, John, ex Bo'ness, sailor, d. 1699 in Darien, reg. 1707. (CC8.8.83)

Clark, William, in Youngston, Ohio, reg. 1877. (SC70.1.184)

Clark, William Bennet, in Texas, reg. 1886. (SC70.1.247)

Clayton, Francis, merchant in Wilmington, North Carolina, reg. 16 May 1791. (CC8.8.128)

Cleghorn, William, in Schley Co, Georgia, reg. 1897. (SC70.1.362)

Cleland, James, ex Edinburgh, merchant, d. 1699 in Darien, reg. 1707. (CC8.8.83)

Clelone, Robert, sailor, d. 1699 in Darien, reg. 1707. (CC8.8.83)

Clintrie, Archibald, sailor, d. 1698 in Darien, reg. 1707. (CC8.8.83)

Clow, Robert, in Oregon Precinct, Illinois, reg. 1874. (SC70.1.167)

Cochrane,Archibald, marblecutter in Ohio, reg. 1891.
    (SC70.1.295)

Cochran, Henry, in Selina, Dallas Co, Alabama, reg. 1889.
    (SC70.1.279)

Cock, David, mariner in Jamaica, reg. 3 Aug. 1799.
    (CC8.8.131)

Cockayne, Francis Henry, in Placer Co, California, reg. 1898.
    (SC70.1.365)

Cockburn, Henry, clergyman in Grenada, d. 19 July 1854,
    reg. 1855.   (SC70.1.55)(F1978)

Cockburn, James, ex Lasswade, sailor, d. 1698 in Darien,
    reg. 1707.   (CC8.8.83)

Cockfield, Thomas Nelson, merchant in St Kitts, reg. 1869.
    (SC70.1.142)

Cogle, David, ex Wick, sailor, d. 1698 in Darien, reg. 1708.
    (CC8.8.84)

Collie, Thomas, clergyman in St Andrews, Jamaica, d. 14 July
    1836, reg. 1839.   (SC70.1.57)(C2096)

Collie, William, ex Aberdeen, in Norfolk, Virginia,
    reg. 1900.   (SC70.1.394)

Collingham, Barnard, in Providence, Rhode Island, reg. 1881.
    (SC70.1.200)

Collins, Jess, in Nipean, Carleton, Canada, reg. 1895.
    (SC70.1.336)

Collymore,Janet, in Barbados, d. Nov. 1843 in Edinburgh.
    (F44)

Colt, Andrew, ex Stirlingshire, mariner, d. 1698 in Darien,
    reg. 1707.   (CC8.8.83)

Colvill, John, mariner, d. 1699 in Darien, reg. 1707.
    (CC8.8.83)

Colville, Thomas Low, in Wilmington, USA, reg. 1875.
    (SC70.1.171)

Colvin, James Kennedy, ironfounder in Providence, Rhode
    Island, reg. 1896.   (SC70.1.350)

Conn, Margaret, in WEstminster, Middlesex, Canada, d. Sep.
    1853, reg. 1855.   (SC70.1.86)(E4226)

Connal, Robert Meiklejohn, in New York, reg. 1892.
    (SC70.1.308)

Connell, Alexander Hutchison, in Montreal, reg. 1898.
    (SC70.1.367)

Connell, Janet, in New York, reg. 1883.   (SC70.1.225)

Connell, Robert Hutchison, in Montreal, reg.1898.
    (SC70.1.367)

Conrodsmeyer, Daniel, trumpeter, d. 1698 in Darien, reg.
    1707.   (CC8.8.83)

Cook, Alexander, sailor, d. 1698 in Darien, reg. 1707.
    (CC8.8.83)

Cook, John, ex Kirkcaldy, sailor, d. 1699 in the West Indies,
    reg. 1707.   (CC8.8.83)

Cook, William, ex Kilwinning, in Battle City, USA,
    reg. 1890.   (SC70.1.286)

Cooper, Esther Ritchie, w of Alexander Dunlop, bank manager,
    in Montego Bay, Jamaica, d. 16 May 1844, reg. 1853.
    (SC70.1.53)(E3556)

Copley, Janet, in New York, d. 27 Nov. 1850, reg. 1854.
    (SC70.1.83)(F1851)

Corbet, John, mariner in New Orleans, reg. 1882.
    (SC70.1.214)

Cordiner, James, ex Paisley, merchant in Rappahannock,
    Virginia, reg.19 Mar. 1724.   (CC8.8.89)

Coulter, Hugh, merchant in Maryland, d. Oct. 1763,
    reg. 19 June 1766.   (CC8.8.120)

Coupar, James, ex Erskine, carpenter, d. 1698 in Darien, reg. 1707. (CC8.8.83)

Coustoun, Robert, ex Stirlingshire, sailor, d. 1698 in Darien, reg. 1707. (CC8.8.83)

Coventry, David Sandeman, s of Rev John Coventry in Kirk Yetholm, in US Navy, reg. 1899. (SC70.1.375)

Cowan, Francis, in San Francisco, d. 12 Jan. 1852, reg. 1853. (SC70.1.79)(E3460)

Cowan, John, clerk or storekeeper in St John, Newfoundland, d. Aug. 1820, reg. 18 July 1822. (CC8.8.148)

Cowie, James, ex Edinburgh, artist in Colorado Springs, USA, reg. 1896. (SC70.1.348)

Crabb, Robert, merchant & planter in Amelia, South Carolina, d. 4 Dec. 1811, reg. 3 Oct. 1827. (CC8.8.151)(B1077)

Crachter, John, ex Newcastle, sailor, d. 1698 in Darien, reg. 1707. (CC8.8.83)

Craich, John, ex Peebles, weaver,d. 1698 in Darien, reg. 1707. (CC8.8.83)

Craig, Angus, in Jamaica, d. 22 Oct. 1841 in Edinburgh. (D1568)

Craig,Andrew, ex Greenock, in Trinidad, d. 10 Sep. 1784, reg. 6 Sep. 1805. (CC8.8.136)

Craig, John, in Woodstock, Ontario, reg. 1897. (SC70.1.357)

Craig, Margaret, in Minnesota, reg. 1895. (SC70.1.344)

Craig, Patrick, ex Kirkwall, seaman, d. 1698 in Darien, reg. 1698. (CC8.8.83)

Craig, Peter, in St Vincent, d. 28 Sep. 1854 in Canterbury, reg. 1854. (SC70.1.85)(E4023)

Craigie, William, in Helena, Montana, reg. 1893.
(SC70.1.316)

Cran, William, in Toronto, reg. 1878. (SC70.1.187)

Crawford, Adam, in La Prairie, Marshall Co, Illinois,
reg. 1891. (SC70.1.296)

Crawford, George, ex Glasgow, merchant in Jamaica, reg.
4 Jan. 1802. (CC8.8.133)

Crawford, James, ex Grangepans, sailor, d. 1699 in Darien,
reg. 1707. (CC8.8.83)

Crawford, James, ex Kirkcaldy, sailor, d. 1699 in Darien,
reg. 1707. (CC8.8.83)

Crawford, Janet, in Sothbridge, Massachusetts, reg. 1886.
(SC70.1.251)

Crawford, John, s of Cornelius Crawford, in Clarendon,
Jamaica, reg. 6 Apr. 1771. (CC8.8.123)

Crawford, William, merchant in Dominica, d. 11 Dec. 1850,
reg. 1865. (SC70.1.127)(H1995)

Cree, Cleland, surgeon at Montego Bay, Jamaica, d. 10 Oct.
1838, reg. 1845. (SC70.1.66)(F148)

Cree,James, in New Mexico, reg. 1891. (SC70.1.298)

Crichton, James, merchant in Prince Edward Island, d. Nov.
1820, reg. 24 Sep. 1824. (CC8.8.150)(SC70.1.31)

Crichton, James Maitland, in Makgill, Jamaica, reg. 1877.
(SC70.1.186)

Croake, Robert, seaman, d. 1698 in Darien, reg. 1707.
(CC8.8.83)

Crooks, James, soldier, d. 1699 in Darien, reg. 1707.
(CC8.8.83)

Crookshanks, Charles, in Baltimore, d. 1800, reg. 29 July
1818. (CC8.8.144)

Crookshanks, William,ex Banff, overseer in St Kitts, d. 1740,
reg. 5 Jan. 1743.   (CC8.8.106)

Crossly, Thomas Baldwin, in East Orange, New Jersey,
reg. 1897.   (SC70.1.355)

Cruickshank, James, in St Vincent, d. 1817, reg. 1831.
(SC70.1.44)(C400)

Crystal, Andrew, ex Auchenleck, farmer in Loth, Lincoln,
Ontario, reg. 1885.   (SC70.1.244)

Cuddie, Jean, w of John Keir, in Philadelphia, reg. 1831.
(SC70.1.44)

Cullen, Isabella, d. 3 Apr. 1834 in Jamaica, reg. 1854.
(SC70.1.62)(F1815)

Cumming, Daniel, ex Edinburgh, sailor, d. 1698 in Darien,
reg. 1707.   (CC8.8.83)

Cumming, Joseph, in Carricou, Grenada, d. 1786, reg.
3 July 1799.   (CC8.8.131)

Cumming, Thomas, ex Culross, sailor, d. 1699 in Darien,
reg. 1707.   (CC8.8.83)

Cumming, William, in Kingston, Jamaica, d. 17 Nov. 1803,
reg. 31 May 1810.   (CC8.8.138)

Cunningham, Alexander, ex Dysart, sailor, d. 1698 in Darien,
reg. 1707.   (CC8.8.83)

Cunningham, Alexander, grocer in New York, reg. 1892.
(SC70.1.311)

Cunningham, George, in Peterboro, Canada, reg. 1866.
(SC70.1.130)

Cunningham, Henry, Governor of Jamaica, d. 173-, reg.
30 Aug. 1739.   (CC8.8.102)

Cunningham, Henry, ex Edinburgh, surgeon in St Augustine,
East Florida, reg. 23 Nov. 1792.   (CC8.8.129)

Currie, Agnes, w of Rev. Adam Thomson, in Jamaica,
    d. 19 Dec. 1850, reg. 1852.   (SC70.1.77)(F1553)

Currie, Agnes, in Jamaica, reg. 1853.   (SC70.1.77)

Currie, Alexander, merchant in Curacao, d. 15 Apr. 1728,
    reg. 1 June 1741.   (CC8.8.104)

Currie, Alexander, in Jamaica, d. Aug. 1828, reg.
    25 Aug. 1829.   (CC8.8.152)

Currie, Alexander, in Tobago, d. Aug. 1828, reg. 1829.
    (SC70.1.41)(D67)

Currie, Francis William, in Ontario, reg. 1896.
    (SC70.1.351)

Currie, John, ex Haddington, merchant in Jamaica, d. 1747,
    reg. 10 Jan. 1785.   (CC8.8.126)

Cussins, John, sailor, d. 1698 in Darien, reg. 1707.
    (CC8.8.83)

Cuthbert, Janet, in Grand Rapids, Michigan, reg. 1874.
    (SC70.1.169)

Cuthbertson, John, blacksmith in Havanna, d. 15 Feb. 1854,
    reg. 1856.   (SC70.1.92)(G340)

D'Albertanson, Adolphus, in Halifax, Nova Scotia,
    d. 14 July 1861, reg. 1863.   (SC70.1.116)(H1430)

Dalgety, Jane Bowhill, in Michaux, Powhatan Co, Virginia,
    reg. 1900. (SC70.1.393)

Dalgleish, Thomas, tinsmith in Canada, reg. 1876.
    (SC70.1.180)

Dall, Robert, in Cedar Valley, Jamaica, reg. 1852.
    (SC70.1.77)

Dallas, James, in Ontario, reg. 1872.   (SC70.1.160)

Dalrymple, William, physician in Jamaica, d. 31 Mar. 1860,
    reg. 1863. (SC70.1.119)(G3263)

Dalziell, Charles, soldier, d. 1699 in Darien, reg. 1707.
    (CC8.8.83)

Daniell, James, judge in Rescott, Ontario, reg. 1891.
    (SC70.1.291)

Darling, David, surgeon in Old Harbor, Middlesex,
    Jamaica, d. 31 Oct. 1840, reg. 1851.   (SC70.1.292)

Daniell, Elizabeth, in Rescott, Ontario, reg. 1891.
    (SC70.1.292)

D'Arusmont, Frances, in Cincinnati, USA, d. 13 Dec. 1852,
    reg. 1853. (SC70.1.141)

Darling, William, in Canada, reg. 1871.   (SC70.1.153)

Davidson, Charles Felix, in Augusta, Maine, reg. 1887.
    (SC70.1.259)

Davidson, David William, merchant in Omaha, Nebraska,
    reg. 1887. (SC70.1.255)

Davidson, Euphemia, in Albany City, USA, reg. 1874.
    (SC70.1.169)

Davidson, Harry, in Falmouth, Jamaica, reg. 1874.
(SC70.1.168)

Davidson, James, surgeon in Jamaica, reg. 1869.
(SC70.1.141)

Davidson, Joseph, ex Ayr, gunner, d. 1698 in Darien,
reg. 1708. (CC8.8.84)

Davidson, Robert, ex Edinburgh, sailor, d. 1698 in
Darien, reg. 1707. (CC8.8.83)

Davidson, William, mariner, d. 1698 in Darien, reg. 1707.
(CC8.8.83)

Dawson, Dougald, manager of Jordanhill Estate, Trinidad,
d. 21 Mar. 1841, reg. 1842. (SC70.1.62)(D1600)

Dawson, William, ex Perth, clergyman in Pensacola,
Florida, reg. 17 Apr. 1770. (CC8.8.121)

Dean, Jane, in Potsdam, St Lawrence Co, New York, reg. 1890.
(SC70.1.286)

De Lancy, James, soldier, US Club, London, d. 26 May 1857,
reg. 1859. (SC70.1.115)(H587)

Denham, Robert, merchant in Savannah, reg. 20 May 1786.
(CC8.8.127)

Denholm, John, surgeon in Grenada, reg. 20 May 1793.
(CC8.8.129)

Dent, William, in Fauquier Co, Virginia, reg. 1886.
(SC70.1.254)

Deuchar, Alexander, clergyman in St Thomas, Barbados,
d. 3 Feb. 1732, reg. 19 Apr. 1738. (CC8.8.100)

Dewar, David, in Massachusetts, reg. 1869. (SC70.1.142)

Dick, Edward, ex Airth, sailor, d. 1698 in Darien, reg.
1707. (CC8.8.83)

Dick, Helen, in Truro, Nova Scotia, reg. 1886.
(SC70.1.251)

Dick, James, merchant in Jamaica, d. 4 Mar. 1824 in London, reg. 1824. (CC8.8.150)(SC70.1.32)

Dick, John, ex Airth, cook, d. 1698 in Darien, reg. 1707. (CC8.8.83)

Dick, Thomas, clerk in Antigua, reg. 1864. (SC70.1.134)

Dick, William, officer of the New York Independent Company of Foot, reg. 9 Oct. 1747. (CC8.8.111)

Dickie, Alexander, ex Ayrshire, in Buffalo, Washington Co, Pennsylvania, reg. 1888. (SC70.1.269)

Dickson, Henry, ex Edinburgh, in Port of Spain, Trinidad, reg. 1869. (SC70.1.143)

Dickson, James, in Brooklyn, New York, reg. 1869. (SC70.1.143)

Dickson, William, in New York, reg. 1869. (SC70.1.144)

Dobson, George, in Green, Adams Co, Ohio, reg. 1889. (SC70.1.272)

Dodd, Thomas Anderson, in Porto Rico, reg. 1897. (SC70.1.364)

Dods, John, engineer in San Fernando, Trinidad, d. 27 Feb. 1865, reg. 1865. (SC70.1.126)(H1928)

Dods, Robert Young, in Porto Rico, reg. 1869. (SC70.1.143)

Dods, William Anderson, in Porto Rico, reg. 1869. (SC70.1.143)

Doig, Paul, in Jamaica, reg. 1847. (SC70.1.67)

Donald, Alexander, ex Greenock, merchant in Virginia, reg. 22 Aug. 1806. (CC8.8.136)

Donald, David, ex Kincardine-on-Forth, sailor, d. 1699 in Darien, reg. 1707. (CC8.8.83)

Donald, David, d. 1699 in Darien, reg. 1709. (CC8.8.84)

Donald, John, ex Kirriemuir, at Montego Bay, Jamaica,
    d. 19 May 1819, reg. 13 Nov. 1819. (CC8.8.145)

Donald, Robert, merchant in Petersburg, Virginia,
    reg. 22 Aug. 1806. (CC8.8.136)

Donaldson, Alexander, planter in Tobago, d. 2 Feb. 1852,
    reg. 1853. (SC70.1.80)(E3514)

Donaldson, James, ex Maybole, in Jamaica, d. 27 Oct. 1828,
    reg. 1833. (SC70.1.49)

Donaldson, Robert, army officer in Ottawa, d. 3 Jan.
    1865, reg. 1865. (SC70.1.127)(G4094)

Donnelly, William, merchant in Harbor Grace, Newfoundland,
    d. 27 Mar. 1864, reg. 1864. (SC70.1.122)(G3581)

Dougall, John, ex Crawforddykes, sailor, d. 1699 in
    Darien, reg. 1707. (CC8.8.83)

Douglas, George, soldier, d. 1699 in Darien, reg. 1707.
    (CC8.8.83)

Douglas, James, ex Edinburgh, carpenter, d. 1698 in
    Darien, reg. 1707. (CC8.8.83)

Douglas, James, in St John, Newfoundland, d. 30 Oct.
    1854, reg. 1855. (SC70.1.54)(D946)

Douglas, John, in Bathurst, USA, d. 11 Mar. 1836, reg.
    1836. (SC70.1.95)(H340)

Douglas, John, ex Castle Douglas, Provost Marshal of
    Grenada, d. 31 Aug. 1838, reg. 1857.
    (SC70.1.95)(H340)

Douglas, John, ex Urray, Ross-shire, in California,
    reg. 1891. (SC70.1.301)

Douglas, Robert, physician in Tobago, d. 17 Apr. 1859,
    reg. 1861. (SC70.1.107)(G2030)

Douglas, William, in Baltimore, reg. 1895.   (SC70.1.338)

Dow, Alexander Drysdale, in Honolulu, reg. 1876.
      (SC70.1.178)

Dow, James, coxswin, d. 1698 in the West Indies, reg. 1707.
      (CC8.8.83)

Downie, James, ex Peterhead, sailor, d. 1698 in Darien,
      reg. 1707.   (CC8.8.83)

Drew, William Carfrae, in Denver, Colorado, reg. 1894.
      (SC70.1.329)

Drummond, Agnes, in Grenada, reg. 1876.   (SC70.1.177)

Drummond, Andrew, in Mocha, Jamaica, d. 4 Jan. 1851,
      reg. 1859.   (SC70.1.100)(E3546)

Drummond, Charles, schoolmaster-sergeant in the 26th
      Cameronians, in Bermuda, d. 20 Mar. 1858, reg. 1858.
      (SC70.1.98)(G1063)

Drummond, James, in New York, d. 21 Feb. 1801, reg. 23
      Apr. 1806.   (CC8.8.136)

Drummond, Robert, in Oneida Co, New York, reg. 1869.
      (SC70.1.143)

Drummond, Thomas, ex Edinburgh, soldier, d. 1699 in Darien,
      reg. 1707.   (CC8.8.83)

Drummond, Thomas, slater in Louisiana, reg. 1890.
      (SC70.1.290)

Dryburgh, Andrew, clergyman in Elmvira, Canada, reg. 1878.
      (SC70.1.188)

Drysdale, David, ex Culross, sailor, d. 1699 in Darien,
      reg. 1707.   (CC8.8.83)

Drysdale, John, in St Louis, Missouri, reg. 1869.
      (SC70.1.143)

Duff, Alexander, in St Vincent, d. Jan. 1819, reg. 13 June
      1823.   (CC8.8.149)

Duffus, Jane, in Princeton, New Jersey, d. 29 Jan. 1858, reg. 1861. (SC70.1.108)(G2160)

Duffy, James, innkeeper in Toronto, reg. 1886. (SC70.1.249)

Duguid, Deidaina, in America, d. 1853, reg. 1856. (SC70.1.92)(H170)

Duguid, Eleanor, in America, d. 1853, reg. 1856. (SC70.1.92)(H170)

Duguid, William, in Pompy, Onandago, New York, d. 13 Mar. 1854, reg. 1856. (SC70.1.92)(G331)

Duncan, Alexander, in Providence, Rhode Island, reg. 1890. (SC70.1.283)

Duncan, Andrew, in Prince Edward Island, d. Apr. 1830, reg. 1830. (SC70.1.42)(C268)

Duncan, Thomas, in Peterborough, Upper Canada, d. 5 Sep. 1854, reg. 1856. (SC70.1.93)(H198)

Duncan, Walter, ex Bo'ness, shipmaster, d. 1699 in Darien, reg. 1707. (CC8.8.83)

Duncan, William, sergeant in 4th Foot, d. in Guadaloupe, reg. 25 July 1762. (CC8.8.117)

Duncanson, John, farmer in Rossburn PO, Bird Trail Creek, Manitoba, reg. 1891. (SC70.1.292)

Dundas, George Younger, in St Vincent, reg. 1881. (SC70.1.212)

Dunlop, Colin McKenzie, in Virginia, reg. 1876. (SC70.1.176)

Dunlop, John Alexander, s of Alexander Dunlop, bank-manager at Montego Bay, Jamaica, d. 16 Sep. 1844, reg. 1853. (SC70.1.80)(F1714)

Dunlop, William, in Cincinnati, reg. 1869. (SC70.1.142)

Dunn, Amelia, in Richmond, New York, reg. 1899.
    (SC70.1.384)

Dunn, John Ritchie, in San Francisco, reg. 1881.
    (SC70.1.210)

Durie, Robert, carpenter in Kansas City, reg. 1893.
    (SC70.1.320)

Duthie, James Cowe, ex Bonnyrig, bricklayer in Denver,
    Colorado, reg. 1887.   (SC70.1.261)

Eadie, George Frederick, in New York, reg. 1866.
(SC70.1.132)

Eagleton, Archibald, ex Edinburgh, sailor, d. 1698 in Darien,
reg. 1707.   (CC8.8.83)

Easton, Thomas, estate manager in St Vincent, reg. 1873,
(SC70.1.163)

Easton, George, merchant in St John, New Brunswick, reg. 1888.
(SC70.1.265)

Eccles, George, merchant in Jamaica, d. 1799, reg. 18 Dec. 1812,
(CC8.8.138)

Eckford, John, in Brant, Canada, reg. 1882.   (SC70.1.213)

Edgar, Alexander, in Jamaica, reg. 1821.   (SC70.1.21)

Edgar, Handasyde, in St James, Cornwall, Jamaica, reg.
8 Apr. 1814.   (CC8.8.140)

Edwards, John, receiver general in Jamaica, d. 18 Jan. 1848,
reg. 1849.   (SC70.1.1869)(E1917)

Elder, John, in Elderslee, Canada, reg. 1880.   (SC70.1.200)

Ellis, Adam Gibb, advocate in Jamaica, reg. 1895
(SC70.1.337)

Ellis, Anthony Hardy, cabinetmaker in Toronto, d. 15 Jul. 1856,
reg. 1856.   (SC70.1.90)(H281)

Emney, Christine, in Murraybay, Canada, d. 10 Apr. 1828, reg
1829.   (SC70.1.39)(C2)

English, Lyman, in Oshawa, Ontario, reg. 1889.   (SC70.1.280)

Erskine, Alexander, plumber in Toronto, reg. 1867.
(SC70.1.134)

Erskine, David, in Montego Bay, Jamaica, reg. 6 Jan. 1798.
(CC8.8.131)

Ewart, Helen, in Kingston, Jamaica, reg. 1891.   (SC70.1.298)

Ewart, Mathilde, in Kingston, Jamaica, reg. 1891.
    (SC70.1.298)

Ewing, James Phin, in Philadelphia, reg. 1895.   (SC70.1.345)

Fair, James, in Port Sarnia, Canada West, d. 8 Dec. 1854,
     reg. 1859. (SC70.1.100)(H594)

Faichney, Ann, ex Perth, in South Carolina, reg. 8 Dec. 1797.
     (CC8.8.130)

Fairbairn, Allan, in Chicago, reg. 1896. (SC70.1.346)

Fairbairn, Henry Brougham, in Chicago, reg. 1896.
     (SC70.1.346)

Fairbairn, James Newell, in Chicago, reg. 1896. (SC70.1.346)

Fairbairn, Maud, in Chicago, reg. 1896. (SC70.1.346)

Fairbairn, Robert, sailor in Darnia, Canada West, reg. 1881.
     (SC70.1.210)≛

Fairbairn, Robert, in Chicago, reg. 1896. (SC70.1.346)

Fairholm, Thomas, ex Edinburgh, merchant in Tobago, d. 7 Feb.
     1791. (CC8.8.128)

Falconer, Archibald Cowan, ex Dalkeith, in Boston, USA, reg.
     1900. (SC70.1.394)

Farms, Margaret, in New Jersey, reg. 1895. (SC70.1.337)

Farquhar, David, merchant in Kingston, Jamaica, d. 1758,
     reg. 7 Apr. 1763. (CC8.8.119)

Farquhar, George Peat, merchant in St Lucia, d. 3 Jan. 1860,
     reg. 1860. (SC70.1.106)(H903)

Farquhar, Jean, in Rosendale, Boston, reg. 1893. (SC70.1.322)

Farquhar, John, ex Edinburgh, merchant in Spanish Town, Jamaica,
     reg. 22 Jun. 1767. (CC8.8.120)

Farquhar, William P, in Storbridge, Worcester, Massachusetts,
     reg. 1882. (SC70.1.215)

Ferguson, Alexander, ex Maybole, soldier, d. 1699 in Darien,
     reg. 1707. (CC8.8.83)

Ferguson, Alexander, in Westmoreland, Jamaica, d. 12 Dec. 1836,
    reg. 1837. (SC70.1.55)(D1020)

Ferguson, Duncan, in Idaho, reg. 1894. (SC70.1.1329)

Ferguson, Henry, ex Edinburgh, clerk, d. 22 Oct. 1859 in New
    Orleans, reg. 1860. (SC70.1.105)(H882)

Ferguson, James, ex Fife, mariner, d. 1698 in Darien, reg. 1707,
    (CC8.8.83)

Ferguson, John, physician in Kingston, Jamaica, reg. 1856.
    (SC70.1.92)

Ferguson, John Proctor, in Chicago, reg. 1900. (SC70.1.393

Ferguson, Robert, in Grenada, reg. Oct. 1793. (CC8.8.129)

Ferguson, Robert, merchant in Wigton, Jamaica, d. 12 Sep. 1855
    in Detroit, reg. 1857. (SC70.1.93)(H221)

Ferguson, Thomas, in Antigua, reg. 1989. (SC70.1.375)

Ferguson, William, in Matanzas, Cuba, d. 16 Aug. 1856, reg.
    1865. (SC70.1.125)(H1870)

Ferguson, William, in Beverly, Burlington County, New Jersey,
    reg. 1884. (SC70.1.230)

Fergusson, Jessie, in Woodhill, Canada, d. 20 Mar. 1856, reg.
    1856. (SC70.1.92)(G296)

Ferrier, Alexander David, in Fergus, Canada, d. Campbelltown,
    Argyll, reg. 1891. (SC70.1.297)

Ferrier, David, attorney in Kingston, Jamaica, d. Mar. 1819
    in Edinburgh, reg. 1855. (SC70.1.88)(E4439)

Ferrier, Julia, in Barrie, Simco County, Ontario, reg. 1890.
    (SC70.1.283)

Ferrier, Louis H, in Quebec, d. 28 Jan. 1833. (C900)

Field, Henry, in Rosser, Manitoba, reg 1894.   (SC70.1.333)

Findlay, Alexander, ex Queensferry, seaman, d. 1699 in Darien,
    reg. 1707.   (CC8.8.83)

Findlay, Arthur Stephen, in St Lucia, reg. 1897.   (SC70.1.358)

Finlay, James Watson, in New Brunswick, reg. 1878.
    (SC70.1.190)

Finlayson, William, ex Stirling, in America, reg. 1707.
    (CC8.8.83)

Finlayson, William Thomas, in Detroit, reg. 1879.   (SC70.1.197)

Fisher, George Barton, in Vancouver City, reg. 1895.
    (SC70.1.340)

Fisher, James, in Jamaica, d. 1789, reg. 4 Oct. 1804.
    (CC8.8.135)

Fisher, James Campbell, clerk in St Kitts, d. Dec. 1853, reg.
    1854.   (SC70.1.83)(F1855)

Fisher, John, in Lennoxville, Quebec, reg. 1899.   (SC70.1.379)

Fleming, Alexander, ex Dysart, sailor, d. 1698 in Darien,
    reg. 1707.   (CC8.8.83)

Fleming, George, mariner, d. 1699 in Darien, reg. 1707.
    (CC8.8.83)

Fleming, Millar, in Drumbo, Ontario, reg. 1897.   (SC70.1.356)

Fletcher, William, ex Edinburgh, in Augusta, Georgia, d. 1836,
    reg. 1856.   (SC70.1.90)(H45)

Flett, William, ex Orkney, in Rupert's Land, d. 11 Nov. 1823,
    reg. 1826.   (CC8.8.151)(SC70.1.34)

Flowerdew, James Gray, merchant in Portland, USA, reg. 1873.
    (SC70.1.165)

Foord, William, ex Burntisland, sailor, d. 1698 in Darien,
    reg. 1707.   (CC8.8.83)

Forbes, Alexander, in Kingston, Jamaica, d. 30 Apr. 1803, reg.
    9 Mar. 1804.   (CC8.8.136)

Forbes, Alexander, merchant in San Francisco, reg. 1884.
    (SC70.1.230)

Forbes, John Stuart, US Army, reg. 1877.   (SC70.1.183)

Forbes, William, ex Aberdeen, in North America, reg. 1890.
    (SC70.1.286)

Ford, John Ross, in New York, reg. 1897.   (SC70.1.357)

Fordyce, Peter, bookkeeper in La Cateaux, Tobago,
    d. 1 Nov. 1830, reg. 1834.   (SC70.1.50)(C974)

Forrest, James, clergyman in Fairmount, West Farm, New York,
    d. 18 FEb. 1858, reg. 1858.   (SC70.1.98)(H493)

Forrest, James, ex Stirling, physician in Ochil Farm, Lake
    Wilson, Minnesota, reg. 1888.   (SC70.1.268)

Forrester, John, in Corosal, Honduras, reg. 1872.
    (SC70.1.157)

Forrester, John Young, in Greensburg, USA, reg. 1869.
    (SC70.1.144)

Forrester, Somerville, in Westmoreland, Cornwall County,
    Jamaica, d. 1 Oct. 1804, reg. 20 Apr. 1811.
    (CC8.8.138)

Forsyth, John, in St Anne, Jamaica, reg. 1854.
    (SC70.1.82)

Forsyth, William, ex Elgin, in New Providence, d. 1797,
    reg. 18 Sep. 1810.   (CC8.8.138)

Forsythe, John, land agent in Chicago, reg. 1886.
    (SC70.1.253)

Fotheringham, Adam, sailor, d. 1698 in Darien, reg. 1707.
    (CC8.8.83)

Fotheringham, James, in New Hampshire, reg. 1877.
    (SC70.1.186)

Fouller, Thomas, ex Greenock, sailor, d. 1698 in Darien,
    reg. 1708.   (CC8.8.84)

Fowles, Allan, in Santa Domingo, reg. 1824.   (SC70.1.31)

Fowles, Archibald Primrose, in Santa Domingo, reg. 1824.
    (SC70.1.31)

Fowles, George, merchant in Santa Domingo, d. Jun. 1820, reg.
    24 Aug. 1824.   (CC8.8.150)(SC70.1.31)

Fowlis, John, carpenter in Morant Bay, Jamaica, reg. 2 Feb.
    1804.   (CC8.8.135)

Frame, Arthur James, physician in Grenada, reg. 1871.
    (SC70.1.153)

Fraser, Alexander, soldier, d. 1699 in Darien, reg. 1708.
    (CC8.8.84)

Fraser, Alexander, ex Newhaven, sailor, d. 1698 in Darien,
    reg. 1708.   (CC8.8.84)

Fraser, Alexander, ex Edinburgh, physician in Annapolis,
    Maryland, reg. 1 Jun. 1732.   (CC8.8.95)

Fraser, Alexander, stonecutter in Toronto, reg. 1880.
    (SC70.1.199)

Fraser, Alexander, ex Glasgow, in New York, reg. 1889.
    (SC70.1.279)

Fraser, Douglas, barrister in Buffalo, New York, reg. 1868.
    (SC70.1.137)

Fraser, Hugh, sailor, d. 1698 in Darien, reg. 1707.
    (CC8.8.83)

Fraser, Hugh, customs collector in Parkham, Antigua, d.
    May 1750, reg. 2 Jul. 1752.   (CC8.8.114)

Fraser, Hugh Grant, in New York, reg. 1893.   (SC70.1.318)

Fraser, Josanna, in Ashtkosh, Wisconsin, reg. 1882.
(SC70.1.214)

Fraser, John, in York, Ontario, reg. 1885. (SC70.1.240)

Fraser, John, ex Edinburgh, nurseryman in Napoleon, Ohio,
reg. 1893. (SC70.1.315)

Fraser, Matthew Moncrieff, ex Glasgow, in Kansas City,
reg. 1885. (SC70.1.239)

Fraser, Rebecca E, in New York, reg. 1887. (SC70.1.260)

Fraser, William, physician in Jamaica, d. Edinburgh, reg.
13 Jul. 1769. (CC8.8.121)

Fraser, William, merchant in Kingston, Jamaica, d. 12 Jun.
1839, reg. 1844. (SC70.1.66)(E286)

Freeland, William, physician in Ottawa, reg. 1873.
(SC70.1.165)

Frigg, Andrew, shipmaster in Jamaica, d. 1769, reg.
28 Apr. 1775. (CC8.8.123)

Fullarton, Philip Khanin, in Port Robinson, Canada West,
reg. 1852. (SC70.1.75)

Fullarton, Thomas, mariner, d. Dec. 1699 in Darien,
reg. 1707. (CC8.8.83)

Fuller, Thomas Brock, in York, Ontario, reg. 1886.
(SC70.1.250)

Fulton, Arthur Rankin, seaman in Jamaica, reg. 1881.
(SC70.1.209)

Fyfe, Charles Gordon, in Jamaica, d. 24 Jul. 1859 in Up Park
Camp, reg. 1863. (SC70.1.118)(H1562)

Fyffe, James, journeyman millwright, in Pennsylvania,
d. 21 Dec. 1856, reg. 1858. (SC70.1.98)(H471)

Fyffe, Mary, in Southbridge, Massachusetts, reg. 1898.
(SC70.1.374)

Fyfe, Walter, coppersmith in Annatto Bay Jamaica, d. May 1821,
reg. 18 Oct. 1824.   (CC8.8.150)

Gairdner, William, ex Abbotshall, sailor, d. 1698 in Darien, reg. 1707. (CC8.8.83)

Galbraith, William, in Jamaica, reg. 23 June 1768. (CC8.8.121)

Galletly, Janet, in New York, reg. 1883. (SC70.1.225)

Gallie, Alexander,d. 1831 in Jamaica, reg. 1858. (SC70.1.90)(H47)

Galloway, John, ex Culross, seaman, d. 1699 in Darien, reg. 1707. (CC8.8.83)

Galloway, John, banker in New York, d. Jan. 1852 in Buchlyvie, Kippen, reg. 1852. (SC70.1.77)(E3212)

Gardner, James, merchant in Jamaica, reg. 22 Oct. 1802. (CC8.8.133)

Garioch, Alexander, ex Edinburgh, stockbroker & merchant in San Francisco, reg. 1889. (SC70.1.276)

Garside, Joseph, in New York, reg. 1888. (SC70.1.265)

Garvie, John, in Mississippi, reg. 1870. (SC70.1.148)

Gascoign, Francis, ex Newcastle, sailor, d. 1698 in Darien,reg. 1707. (CC8.8.83)

Gavin, John, in Poughkeepsie, New York, reg. 1891. (SC70.1.296)

Geddes, John, station agent in USA, reg. 1894. (SC70.1.331)

George, James, in Toronto, reg. 1879. (SC70.1.193)

Gibb, Alexander, station agent for Grand Trunk Railroad, Ontario, reg. 1884. (SC70.1.235)

Gibb, Christina, in Camp Hall, Virginia, d. 30 Mar. 1861, reg. 1864. (SC70.1.121)(H1693)

Gibb, James, ex Abercorn, sailor, d. 1699 in Darien,
    reg. 1707.   (CC8.8.83)

Gibb, John, ex Bo'ness, sailor, d. 1698 in Darien,
    reg. 1707.   (CC8.8.83)

Gibb, William, merchant in San Francisco, reg. 1872.
    (SC70.1.160)

Gibson, Alexander, ex Selkirk, d. 11 Oct. 1861 in
    America, reg. 1862.   (SC70.1.111)(H1189)

Gibson, Eliza Finch, in Antigua, reg. 1867.   (SC70.1.136)

Gibson, George, ex Edinburgh, surgeon, d. 1699 in Darien,
    reg. 1707.   (CC8.8.83)

Gibson, James, stationer in Montrel, d. 11 July 1849,
    reg. 1851.   (SC70.1.70)(F1040)

Gibson, James, ex Prestonpans, sailor, d. 1698 in Darien,
    reg. 1707.   (CC8.8.83)

Gibson, James, clergyman in New York, reg. 1860.
    (SC70.1.106)

Gibson, Malcolm, surgeon, d. 1699 in Darien, reg. 1707.
    (CC8.8.83)

Gibson, William, merchant in St Thomas, d. 14 June 1841,
    reg. 1842.   (SC70.1.61)(C2776)

Gibson, William, writer in Montreal, reg. 1893.
    (SC70.1.321)

Gilchrist, Andrew, ex Glasgow, merchant in Accomack Co,
    Virginia, d. 17...   (CC9.7.62)

Gilchrist, Henry, ex Burntisland, seaman, d. 1698 in
    Darien, reg. 1707.   (CC8.8.83)

Gilchrist, Margaret, in Montreal, reg. 1891.   (SC70.1.295)

Gilchrist, Robert, ex Duns, merchant in Barbados, d. 1649,
    reg. 1653.   (CC8.8.67)

Gillespie, George Hamilton, in Hamilton, Ontario, reg. 1900.   (SC70.1.394)

Gillespie, James, in St Vincent, reg. 1821.   (SC70.1.23)

Gillespie, James, in Boston, reg. 1898.   (SC70.1.374)

Gillespie, William, ex Edinburgh, d. 1812 in Jamaica, reg. 1859.   (SC70.1.   )(H750)

Gillies, Robert, officer in the American Provincial Corps, reg. 7 June 1783.   (CC8.8.125)

Gilmour, James, in Mound, USA, reg. 1882.   (SC70.1.214)

Gilmour, John, mariner, d. 1699 in Darien, reg. 1707. (CC8.8.83)

Gilmour, John, clergyman in Canada, reg. 1869. (SC70.1.146)

Ginty, John, contractor in New York, reg. 1885. (SC70.1.239)

Girvan, Thomas, engineer in Surrey, Jamaica, reg. 1889. (SC70.1.278)

Givein, Robert, ex Leith, sailor, d. 1698 in Darien, reg. 1707.   (CC8.8.83)

Glass, George, in Jamaica, d. Edinburgh, reg. 29 Dec. 1796, (CC8.8.130)

Glass, James Duncan, in California, reg. 1899. (SC70.1.379)

Glen, Duncan, ex Edinburgh, steward, d. 1698 in Darien, reg. 1707.   (CC8.8.83)

Glen, William, in Westmoreland, Jamaica, d. 17 Sep. 1845, reg. 1851.   (SC70.1.73)

Glover, Alexander Johnston, in Washington, reg. 1896. (SC70.1.348)

Goalen, Alexander James, ex Edinburgh, d. in the West
    Indies, reg. 1890. (SC70.1.283)

Goldie, Catherine, w of Andrew Newton customs-controller,
    Accomack, Virginia, reg. 17 Oct. 1788. (CC8.8.127)

Goodfellow, Robert, in Jamaica, d. 23 Nov. 1827, reg.
    30 Aug. 1828. (CC8.8.152)(SC70.1.39)(B1367)

Goodlet, Jane, ex Musselburgh, in New York, d. 2 Jan. 1836,
    reg. 1838. (SC70.1.56)(D1071)

Gordon, Alexander, planter in Jamaica, d. 178-, reg.
    17 Nov. 1783. (CC8.8.126)

Gordon, Alexander, in St Croix, d.24 Jan. 1805, reg.
    26 July 1806. (CC8.8.136)

Gordon, Alexander, ex Banffshire, in Ancaster, Canada,
    d. 4 Mar. 1838, reg. 1845. (SC70.1.66)(F150)

Gordon, Alexander, in Toronto, reg. 1871. (SC70.1.151)

Gordon, Francis,merchant in Yeocomico, Virginia, reg.
    23 Apr. 1770. (CC8.8.121)

Gordon, George, in Hanover, Jamaica, reg. 13 Dec. 1781.
    (CC8.8.125)

Gordon, James, quartermaster, d. 1698 in Darien, reg. 1707.
    (CC8.8.83)

Gordon, James, in Jersey City, USA, reg. 1890.
    (SC70.1.283)

Gordon, Randolph Norman, in Jamaica, reg. 1894. (SC70.1.330)

Gordon, Walter, overseer at Airy Castle, Jamaica, d. 1782,
    reg. 16 May 1783. (CC8.8.126)

Gordon, William, ex Peterhead, in Jamaica, reg. 16 May 1783.
    (CC8.8.126)

Gordon of Aberdour, William, in St Kitts, reg. 18 June 1840.
     (C2511)

Govan, James, ex Greenock, glasscutter in Mobile, USA,
     d. Sep. 1849, reg. 1855.   (SC70.1.87)(F2070)

Gowan, John, in Crysler, North Finch, Stormont, Canada
     West, d. 19 Jan. 1862, reg. 1863.   (SC70.1.114)(H1369)

Gracie, Mary, in Virginia, d. 11 June 1829 in Edinburgh.
     (C237)

Graham, James, ex Edinburgh, mariner, d. 1698 in Darien,
     reg. 1707.   (CC8.8.83)

Graham, James, ex Glasgow, manufacturer in Trinidad,
     d. 1806.   (CC9.7.79)

Graham, Robert, in Dominica, d. Nov. 1780, reg. 27 Sep.
     1808.   (CC8.8.137)

Graham, William Leckie, ex Glasgow, merchant, d. 16 June
     1843 in St Thomas.   (C3211)

Grahame, Peter, overseer in Windsor, Jamaica, d. Sep.
     1755, reg. 12 Mar. 1776.   (CC8.8.123)

Grainger, James, physician in St Kitts, reg. 8 Apr. 1790.
     (CC8.8.128)

Grant, Ann Ferguson, in Santa Barbara, California, reg.
     1892.   (SC70.1.307)

Grant, David William, in New York, d. 27 Feb. 1838 in
     Edinburgh.   (D1210)

Grant, Donald Fraser, in Newport, Rhode Island, reg. 1884.
     (SC70.1.231)

Grant, George, ex Prestonpans, sailor, d. 1699 in Darien,
     reg. 1707.   (CC8.8.83)

Grant, George, surgeon in Jamaica, d. 1801, reg. 9 Mar.
     1802.   (CC8.8.133)

Grant, Jane, wid. of Kenelon Connor Chandler, in Nicolet, Canada, d. 1 May 1862 in Bristol, reg. 1864. (SC70.1.121)(G3484)

Grant, Jane Calder, in New York, reg. 1893. (SC70.1.320)

Grant, John, Commissary of Ordnance in New York, reg. 23 May 1789. (CC8.8.128)

Grant, John, in Jamaica, d. Mar. 1791, reg. 5 Feb. 1794. (CC8.8.129)

Grant, Peter, yeoman in Cumberland, Canada, reg. 1882. (SC70.1.214)

Grant, Thomas, ex Edinburgh, butcher, d. 1699 in Darien, reg. 1707. (CC8.8.83)

Grant, William Forsyth, physician in Jamaica, d. 2 Aug. 1833, reg. 1835. (SC70.1.52)(C1316)

Gray, Alexander, in Trinidad, d. 20 Aug. 1860 in London, reg. 1864. (SC70.1.121)(G3512)

Gray, Ann, in Missouri, reg. 1898. (SC70.1.369)

Gray, Charles, planter in Tobago, d. 12 Sep. 1826, reg. 1827. (CC8.8.151)(B1151)

Gray, John, merchant in Port Royal, Virginia, d. 1790, reg. 16 May 1791. (CC8.8.128)

Green, John, in Petrsburg, Virginia, d. Edinburgh, reg. 5 July 1797. (CC8.8.130)

Green, Joseph, in Kingston, Jamaica, d. 14 Apr. 1847, reg. 1851. (SC70.1.70)(F1119)

Greenfield, James, ex Stornaway, clergyman in New York, reg. 1900. (SC70.1.388)

Greg, Thomas, ex St Andrews, d. 1699 in the West Indies, reg. 1707. (CC8.8.83)

Greig, Alexander. physician & surgeon in Jamaica, reg.
    23 Feb. 1776.   (CC8.8.124)

Grey, Martin, in Milwaukee, Wisconsin, reg. 1899.
    (SC70.1.385)

Grierson, Joseph, in Greenpark, Jamaica, d. 8 Oct. 1849,
    reg. 1851.   (SC70.1.71)(F1156)

Grieve, James, in Waterdown, Canada, reg. 1889.
    (SC70.1.279)

Grieve, Walter, in Waterdown, Wentworth Co, Ontario,
    reg. 1889.   (SC70.1.277)

Grieve, William, ex Leith, sailor, d. 1699 in Darien,
    reg. 1707.   (CC8.8.83)

Grindlay, John, s of James Grindlay attorney in Charleston,
    South Carolina, clergyman in Lambeth, Surrey, reg.
    10 Oct. 1806.   (CC9.7.79)

Grintoun, Alexander, ex Bo'ness, sailor, d. Darien, reg.
    30 Mar. 1700.   (CC8.8.81)

Gruer, John, in Meagher, Montana, reg. 1898.
    (SC70.1.366)

Guild, Alexander, merchant in New York, reg. 1894.
    (SC70.1.333)

Guthrie, James, ex Largo, mariner, d. 1699 in Darien,
    reg. 1707.   (CC8.8.83)

Haig, Susan, in Port Hope, Canada, reg. 1885.
(SC70.1.243)

Haig, Susan McEwan, in Charleston, South Carolina, reg.
1883. (SC70.1.226)

Hale, Carrie Barton, in Santa Barbara, California, reg.
1894. (SC70.1.336)

Hale, Daniel Horatio, broker in Los Angeles, reg. 1888.
(SC70.1.265)

Haliburton, Thomas, merchant in St Eustatia, d. 179-,
reg. 29 Sep. 1795. (CC8.8.130)

Halkett, John, sailor, d. 1699 in Darien, reg. 1707.
(CC8.8.83)

Hall, Archibald Glen, metal-merchant in Montreal, reg.
1867. (SC70.1.135)

Hally, James, clergyman in Quebec, reg. 1894.
(SC70.1.329)

Hallyburton, William, soldier, d. 1699 in Darien, reg.
1707. (CC8.8.83)

Hamilton, Alexander, ex Bo'ness, mariner, d. 1699 in
Darien, reg. 1707. (CC8.8.83)

Hamilton, Alexander, ex Bo'ness, councillor, d. 1699 in
Darien, reg. 1707. (CC8.8.83)

Hamilton, Alexander, ex Inveresk, mariner, d. 1698 in
Darien, reg. 1707. (CC8.8.83)

Hamilton, Archibald, ex Carriden, sailor, d. 1699 in
Darien, reg. 1707. (CC8.8.83)

Hamilton, Archibald, in Kingston, Jamaica, d. 1799, reg.
9 Mar. 1801. (CC8.8.132)

Hamilton, Caroline, in Niagara, USA, reg. 1899.
(SC70.1.384)

Hamilton, Charles, ex Edinburgh, d. 1698 in Darien, reg.
1707. (CC8.8.83)

Hamilton, David, in Chicago, reg. 1889.   (SC70.1.275)

Hamilton, James, ex Edinburgh, sailor, d. 1699 in Darien,
    reg. 1707. (CC8.8.83)

Hamilton, James, s of William Hamilton in Smailholemill,
    surgeon in New York, reg. 22 Mar. 1781.   (CC8.8.126)

Hamilton, John, in Jamaica, reg. 7 Aug. 1786.   (CC8.8.127)

Hamilton, John, in Montreal, reg. 1888.   (SC70.1.269)

Hamilton, John Robert, in New York, reg. 1876.   (SC70.1.179)

Hamilton, John Stuart, ex Leith, in Coatzacoalos, Mexico,
    reg. 1900.   (SC70.1.394)

Hamilton, Robert, merchant in Jamaica, d. 15 Aug. 1840 in
    London.   (C2482)

Hamilton, Robert, in Douglas, Scarborough, Canada West,
    d. 2 Apr. 1857.   (G643)

Hamilton, Robert D, in Canada, reg. 1857.   (SC70.1.95)

Hamilton, Robert Douglas, in Hamilton, Canada, reg. 1860.
    (SC70.1.105)

Hamilton, Thomas, ex Edinburgh, overseer, d. 1698 in
    Darien, reg. 1707.   (CC8.8.83)

Hamilton, Thomas, ex Bathgate, overseer, d. 1699 in Darien,
    reg. 1707.   (CC8.8.83)

Hamilton, Walter, apothecary in Honduras, d. Ayrshire,
    reg. 28 Apr. 1803.   (CC9.7.588)

Hamilton, William, ex Fife, sailor, d. 1698 in Darien, reg.
    1707.   (CC8.8 .83)

Hamilton, William, in New York, reg. 1825.   (SC70.1.33)

Hamilton, William, in Mobile, Alabama, d. 25 May 1862,
     reg. 1865. (SC70.1.126)(H1918)

Hamilton, William, in Dalhousie, Restigouche, New Brunswick,
     reg. 1888. (SC70.1.267)

Hampstead, James, seaman in the WestIndies, reg. 1869.
     (SC70.1.143)

Handiesyde, James, ex Edinburgh, mariner, d. 1698 in Darien,
     reg. 1707. (CC8.8.83)

Hannah, Mary, in Chicago, reg. 1896. (SC70.1.315)

Hannay, Patrick, in Caldons, Virginia, reg. 1823.
     (SC70.1.28)

Hanson, James, in New York, reg. 1899. (SC70.1.379)

Hardin, Elizabeth, in Brooklyn, New York, reg. 1882.
     (SC70.1.215)

Hardman, James, in Montreal, reg. 1876. (SC70.1.176)

Hardman, Moritz, in St George, Grenada, reg. 1818.
     (SC70.1.17)

Hardy, James, ex Kinneil, sailor, d. 1699 in Darien,
     reg. 1707. (CC8.8.83)

Harkness, James, teacher in Portage, Canada, d. 23 Aug.
     1841, reg. 1845. (CC8.8.148)(SC70.1.24)

Harley, David, in Montreal, reg. 1870. (SC70.1.150)

Harley, John, moulder in Jersey City, USA, d. 11 Nov.
     1848, reg. 1849. (SC70.1.69)

Harper, David, ex Kirkcaldy, mariner, d. 1698 in Darien,
     reg. 1707. (CC8.8.83)

Harper, Robert, soldier, d. 16 Apr. 1828 in Jamaica.
     (D397)

Harris, John Rennie, merchant in Trinidad, reg. 1898.
(SC70.1.369)

Hart, George, master mariner in Newfoundland, reg. 1866.
(SC70.1.131)

Hart, James William, in San Francisco, reg. 1900.
(SC70.1.386)

Hart, Margaret, w of Robert Clark, in Halifax, Nova
Scotia, reg. 30 May 1787. (CC8.8.127)

Hawley, William, in Boston, reg. 1899. (SC70.1.385)

Hay, Andrew, ex Dysart, sailor, d. 1698 in Darien, reg.
1707. (CC8.8.83)

Hay, Duncan, ex Kinloch Dall, weaver in Gross Isle, Lower
Canada, d. 1847, reg. 1852. (SC70.1.74)(F1364)

Hay, Hugh, ex Nairn, soldier, d. 1698 in Darien, reg.
1707. (CC8.8.83)

Hay, John, soldier, d. 1698 in Darien, reg. 1707.
(CC8.8.83)

Hay, Margaret, in Barbados, d. 28 Jan. 1828. (B1232)

Hay, Patrick, ex Edinburgh, overseer, d. 1698 in Darien,
reg. 1707. (CC8.8.83)

Hay, William, ex Edinburgh, sailor, d. 1699 in Darien,
reg. 1707. (CC8.8.83)

Haynes, Richard, in Barbados, d. 15 Nov. 1859 in Bristol,
reg. 1860. (SC70.1.104)(G1696)

Hazel, John, in Kingston, Jamaica, d. 14 May 1820 in Ayr,
reg. 19 Oct. 1820. (CC9.7.81)

Heatly, Edward, in San Francisco, reg. 1899. (SC70.1.384)

Hedderwick, John, ex Aberdeen, sailor, d. 1698 in Darien,
reg. 1708. (CC8.8.84)

Hedderwick, William, ex Edinburgh, surgeon, d. 1699 in
    Darien, reg. 1707.   (CC8.8.83)

Henderson, Charles, planter in Jamaica, d. 12 June 1850,
    reg. 1864.   (SC70.1.123)(H1792)

Henderson, Donald, overseer in Alexandria, Jamaica,
    d. DEc. 1828, reg. 1830.   (SC70.1.42)(D185)

Henderson, Elizabeth Dickson, in Morton, Kingston,
    Ontario, reg. 1890.   (SC70.1.289)

Henderson, Francis Hardie, ex Hawick, soldier, d. 7 Oct.
    1835 in Dominica.   (D1187)

Henderson, James, surgeon & merchant in Kingston, Jamaica,
    d. 18 Apr. 1755, reg. 2 Jan. 1756.   (CC8.8.116)

Henderson, James, in Grenada, d. Greenock, reg. 3 July
    1819.   (CC9.7.83)

Henderson, Jane, at Anotto River Plantation, Jamaica,
    d. 29 May 1829, reg. 1854.   (SC70.1.85)(F1958)

Henderson, John, ex Edinburgh, saddler in Jamaica,
    d. 1755.   (CC8.8.116)

Henderson, Katherine Gray, in Strongsville, Ohio,
    reg. 1880.   (SC70.1.204)

Henderson, Robert, in Alleghany City, Pennsylvania,
    reg. 1888.   (SC70.1.264)

Henderson, William, ex Edinburgh, overseer, d. 1699 in
    Darien, reg. 1707.   (CC8.8.83)

Hendry, Alexander, ex Linlithgow, sailor, d. 1699 in
    Darien, reg. 1707.   (CC8.8.83)

Hendry, Louisa, in Boston, reg. 1893.   (SC70.1.326)

Henry, Louisa Stewart, in Boston, reg. 1889.   (SC70.1.275)

Hepburn, Charles, ex Glasgow, merchant at Cape Fear, North
    Carolina, d. July 1741, reg. 18 May 1744. (CC8.8.107)

Herd, Walter, mariner, d. 1698 in Darien, reg. 1707.
    (CC8.8.83)

Herman, Matthew, seaman, d. 1698 in Darien, reg. 1707.
    (CC8.8.83)

Heugh, Andrew, planter in Montgomery Co, Maryland,
    d. 6 Jan. 1771, reg. 22 June 1791. (CC8.8.128)

Hill, Archibald, storekeeper in Ashkum, Iroquois, USA,
    d. 15 Aug. 1858, reg. 1859. (SC70.1.100)(G1258)

Hill, Charles, officer, d. Darien, reg. 15 Oct. 1700.
    (CC8.8.81)

Hill, George, in Boston, reg. 1879. (SC70.1.195)

Hill, Marion, in La Chine, Canada, reg. 1891. (SC70.1.291)

Hill, Missall Stodart, in Boston, reg. 1878. (SC70.1.189)

Hill, Thomas, farmer in Brock, Canada West, reg. 1869.
    (SC70.1.142)

Hodge, Elizabeth, wid of Ebenezer Reid, in Kingston,
    Jamaica, d. 13 Mar. 1845, reg. 1846. (SC70.1.67)(F409)

Hogan, Mary Susanna, in Cincinatti, reg. 1887. (SC70.1.256)

Hogarth, James, in Victoria, British Columbia, reg. 1900.
    (SC70.1.395)

Hogg, Mark, ex Bonhardpans, sailor, d. 1699 in Darien,
    reg. 1707. (CC8.8.83)

Holbrook, Deidama, in America, d. 1853, reg. 1856.
    (SC70.1.92)(H171)

Holbrook, Eleanor, in America, d. 1853, reg. 1856.
    (SC70.1.92)(H170)

Holland, William, ex Ayr, sailor, d. 1699 in Darien,
    reg. 1708. (CC8.8.84)

Holmes, John J, dyer in Willimankie, Windham Co,
    Connecticut, reg. 1888. (SC70.1.268)

Home, James, s of James Home shipmaster in Leith, in
    Greta, Black River, Mosquito Shore, reg. 29 July
    1785. (CC8.8.127)

Home, William, merchant in Brooklyn, reg. 1892.
    (SC70.1.312)

Hood, David, in Ridgeville, America, reg. 1860.
    (SC70.1.109)

Hood, Matthew, ex Glasgow, carpenter in Tobago, d. 10 May
    1824, reg. 30 Sep. 1825. (CC8.8.150)(SC70.1.33)

Hope, Charles Cowan, in Montreal, reg. 1900. (SC70.1.395)

Hope. Thomas, soldier, d. 1699 in Jamaica, reg. 1707.
    (CC8.8.83)

Horseman, Robert, ex Burghmuirhead, in Poppleton, New York,
    d. 21 Aug. 1799, reg. 5 Aug. 1802. (CC8.8.133)

Hosack, William, in Jamaica, d. Edinburgh, reg. 1885.
    (SC70.1.245)

Houliston, Thomas, in Three Rivers, Upper Canada, reg. 1889.
    (SC70.1.277)

Houstoun, Agnes, in Jamaica, reg. 1853. (SC70.1.77)

Houstoun, Helen, in Illinois, reg. 1894. (SC70.1.334)

Houstoun, William, ex Donegal, sailor, d. 1699 in Darien,
    reg. 1708. (CC8.8.84)

Houstoun, William, in Bellemont Estate, Grenada, d. 2 May
    1843, reg. 1843. (SC70.1.64)(C3151)

Howat, Alexander, in Kirkpatrick, Canada West, reg. 1867.
    (SC70.1.133)

Howie,John, merchant in Kingston, Jamaica, d. 9 Sep. 1847,
    reg. 1849.   (SC70.1.69)(E1451)

Howison, Alexander Preston, in America, reg. 1823.
    (SC70.1.27)

Huddleston, Hugh, ex Canongate, merchant in Jamaica,
    reg. 3 Sep. 1763.   (CC8.8.119)

Huggins, Henry, in USA, reg. 1887.   (SC70.1.262)

Huie, James, mariner in Dumfries, Virginia, reg. 1816.
    (SC70.1.14)

Hull, Ruth, ex Dundee, in New Jersey, reg. 1893.
    (SC70.1.316)

Hunter, John, manager in Montreal, reg. 1892. (SC70.1.299)

Hunter, Margaret, wid of Walter Miller merchant in Jamaica,
    d. 18 Dec. 1847 in Granton,reg. 1852.   (SC70.1.77)

Hunter, Robert, ex Perth, baker, d. 1703 in Darien, reg.
    1707.   (CC8.8.84)

Hunter, Robert Cathcart, soldier in Montreal, d. Aug. 1834.
    (C1304)

Hunter, Thomas, in Woodlawn, Lochore, Amelia Co,
    Virginia, reg. 1884.   (SC70.1.237)

Hussie, Michael, sailor, d. 1698 in Darien, reg. 1707.
    (CC8.8.83)

Hutcheson, Alexander Gordon, in Hilo, Hawaii, reg. 1896.
    (SC70.1.353)

Hutchison, Alexander, sailor, d. 1699 in Darien, reg. 1707.
    (CC8.8.83)

Hutchison, David, ex Dundee, grocer in Chicago, d. 3 Nov.
1854, reg. 1855. (SC70.1.89)(E4504)

Hutchison, James, merchant at the Bay of Honduras,
d. 179-, reg. 12 Dec. 1796. (CC8.8.130)

Hutton, James, ex Kinross, sailor, d. 1698 in Darien,
reg. 1707. (CC8.8.83)

Hutton, John, ex Berwickshire, clergyman, d. 1698 in
Darien, reg. 1707. (CC8.8.83)

Hutton, William Dalgleish, in Jones Co, Iowa, reg. 1899.
(SC70.1.379)

Hyslop, Jean, in Jamaica, d. 9 Nov. 1811, reg. 19 Sep. 1817.
(CC8.8.143)

Imrie, Duncan, ex Dundee, carpenter in St Augstine, East Florida, reg. 26 Sep. 1782. (CC8.8.125)

Imrie, William Beck, in Richmond, Quebec, reg. 1876.

Inches, Andrew, in Frederickton, York, Canada, reg. 1898. (SC70.1.369)

Inglis, Alexander, s of Robert Inglis in Edinburgh, goldsmith in St Kitts, reg. 11 June 1752. (CC8.8.116)

Inglis, Charles, ex St Andrews, sailor, d. 1698 in Darien, reg. 1707. (CC8.8.83)

Inglis, Henry, ex Kinghorn, sailor, d. 1698 in Darien, reg. 1707. (CC8.8.83)

Inglis, James, ex Calder, overseer, d. 1699 in Darien, reg. 1707. (CC8.8.83)

Inglis, James, ex Clackmannan, officer in the Maryland Loyalists, reg. 6 Dec. 1785. (CC8.8.127)

Inglis, Robert, ex St Andrews, sailor, d. 1699 in Darien, reg. 1707. (CC8.8.83)

Ingram, Isaac, in America, reg. 1874. (SC70.1.168)

Ingram, William Alexander, in Chicago, reg. 1900. (SC70.1.395)

Innes, Alexander, ex West Lothian, gunner, d. 1698 in Darien, reg. 1707. (CC8.8.83)

Innes, Frances, da of Alexander Innes surgeon, w of Andrew Buchanan merchant in St Kitts, d. Jan. 1785 in Glasgow, reg. 22 Sep. 1802. (CC9.7.78)

Inslee, William, in Newark, NewJersey, reg. 1898. (SC70.1.376)

Irvine, Charles, in Tobago, d. 11 Apr. 1798, reg. 2 Sep. 1799. (CC8.8.131)

Irvine, Walter, in Tobago, reg. 1825.   (SC70.1.33)

Irving, John, in Nassau, Bahamas, d. 7 Apr. 1840,
     reg. 1840.   (SC70.1.60)(D1420)

Isaac, Alexander, ex Fife, sailor, d. 1698 in Darien,
     reg. 1707.   (CC8.8.83)

Izat, John, ex Alloa, ships carpenter in Charleston,
     South Carolina, d. 1800, reg. 15 Feb. 1804.
     (CC8.8.135)

Izatt, Robert, in Milwaukee, Wisconsin, reg. 1900.
     (SC70.1.393)

Jack, Mary, in Montreal, reg. 1890. (SC70.1.286)

Jackson, George, tinplateworker in Charleston, USA,
    reg. 1866. (SC70.1.129)

Jackson, Isaac, in Copse Estate, Hanover, Jamaica, d. 3 Aug.
    1856, reg. 1857. (SC70.1.94)(G3543)

Jackson, James, ex Edinburgh, sailor, d. 1699 in Darien,
    reg. 1707. (CC8.8.83)

Jackson, John, in St Paul, Ramsay Co, Minnesota, reg. 1885.
    (SC70.1.238)

Jacoby, William, merchant in Masaya, Nicaragua, reg. 1882.
    (SC70.1.213)

Jamieson, James, ex Burntisland, sailor, d. 1698 in Darien,
    reg. 1707. (CC8.8.83)

Jamieson, James, surgeon & merchant in Tobago, reg.
    22 Nov. 1783. (CC8.8.126)

Jamieson, James Ferguson, merchant in Trinidad, reg. 1868.
    (SC70.1.140)

Jamieson, John, in Montreal, reg. 1848. (SC70.1.68)

Jamieson, Thomas Henry, in Buffalo, New York, reg. 1891.
    (SC70.1.296)

Janson, Peter, seaman, d. 1698 in Darien, reg. 1707.
    (CC8.8.83)

Jardine, John, ex Beattock, farmer in Hamilton, Upper
    Canada, reg. 1884. (SC70.1.234)

Jazdowski, Jessie, in Winnipeg, reg. 1884. (SC70.1.230)

Jefferson, Georgina, in Chicago, reg. 1892. (SC70.1.307)

Jelly, William, ex Kirkcudbrightshire, cartwright in
    Salem, Massachusetts, d. Nov. 1813, reg. 22 Nov. 1821.
    (CC8.8.147)

Johnston, Adam, overseer in St Elizabeth's, Jamaica,
    d. July 1795, reg. 12 Mar. 1796.   (CC8.8.130)

Johnston, Alexander, soldier, d. 1699 in Darien,
    reg. 1707.   (CC8.8.83)

Johnstone, Andrew, merchant in Petersburg, Virginia,
    reg. 1788.   (CC8.8.127)

Johnstone, Hugh, planter in Antigua, d. 13 Apr. 1862,
    reg. 1862.   (SC70.1.113)(H1292)

Johnston, James, ex Queensferry, mariner, d. 1698 in Darien,
    reg. 1707.   (CC8.8.83)

Johnston, James, ex Leith, sailor, d. 1698 in Darien,
    reg. 1707.   (CC8.8.83)

Johnston, John, weaver, d. 1699 in Darien, reg. 1707.
    (CC8.8.83)

Johnstone, John, in Kingston, Jamaica, d. 21 May 1828 in
    Edinburgh.   (C89)

Johnstone, Jessie, in New Orleans, reg. 1892.   (SC70.1.310)

Johnstone, Margaret Elizabeth, ex Edinburgh, in Nelson,
    British Columbia, reg. 1900.   (SC70.1.392)

Johnstone, Thomas, ex Dumfries-shire, in Jamaica, d. Dec.
    1830.   (D600)

Johnston, Thomas,merchant in New Orleans, reg. 1866.
    (SC70.1.132)

Johnston, Walter, surgeon, d. 1699 in Darien, reg. 1707.
    (CC8.8.83)

Johnstone, Walter, ex Moffat, surgeon in America, reg. 1887.
    (SC70.1.256)

Kay, William, missionary catechist in Jamaica, d. Oct. 1841, reg. 1842. (SC70.1.62)(D1619)

Kean, Sarah, in Nassagaweya, Canada, reg. 1880. (SC70.1.200)

Kedslie, John, in Washington, USA, d. 14 Apr. 1847, reg. 1848. (SC70.1.68)(F638)

Keir, Jean, in Philadelphia, reg. 1831. (SC70.1.44)

Keith, Jean, in Rosendale, Boston, reg. 1893. (SC70.1.322)

Keith, Robert, mariner, d. 1699 in Darien, reg. 1707. (CC8,8.83)

Kelly, Ann, in Paterson, New Jersey, reg. 1891. (SC70.1.291)

Kelso, Archibald, sailor, d. 1698 in Darien, reg. 1707. (CC8.8.83)

Kennan, William, attorney in Richmond, Virginia, reg. 30 Dec. 1768. (CC8.8.120)

Kennedy, John, in Beaver Falls, Pennsylvania, reg. 1885. (SC70.1.244)

Kennedy, Robert, clergyman in Cheltenham, Canada, reg. 1876. (SC70.1.166)

Kent, William Ralph, in Ottawa, reg. 1876. (SC70.1.181)

Kenyon, Henry, in Boston, USA, d. 23 Mar. 1855, reg. 1856. (SC70.1.90)

Kerr, Jane Calder, in New York, reg. 1893. (SC70.1.320)

Kerr, John, s of Ninian Kerr farmer in Beith, in Henrico Co, Virginia, reg. 20 June 1776. (CC9.7.70)

Kerr, Thomas, engineer, d. 1699 in the West Indies, reg. 1707. (CC8.8.83)

Kerr, William, in Manchester, Virginia, d. 1812 in Ayr, reg. 6 Jan. 1813. (CC9.7.81)

Kerr, William, in Greenwood, Jamaica, reg. 1899. (SC70.1.381)

Kidston, Alexander, in Jamaica, d. 15 Aug. 1850 in Edinburgh, reg. 1850. (SC70.1.71)(E2366)

Kilgour, Alexander, ex Lochgelly, sailor, d. 1698 in Darien, reg. 1709. (CC8.8.84)

Kilpatrick, George, in Louisville, USA, reg. 1869. (SC70.1.143)

King, Horatio, in Washington, DC, reg. 1898. (SC70.1.368)

King, Hugh, millwright in Jamaica, d. 1740, reg. 3 Feb. 1744. (CC8.8.108)

King, John, in Martinique, d. Dec. 1787, reg. 28 Dec. 1824. (CC8.8.150)

King, John, ex Port Glasgow, in St Pierre, Martinique, d. Dec. 1799, reg. 3 Mar. 1807. (CC8.8.137)

King, William Simpson, ex Aberdeen, carpenter in New York, reg. 1900. (SC70.1.396)

Kinneir, Alexander, ex Edinburgh, sailor, d. 1698 in Darien, reg. 1708. (CC8.8.84)

Kinnell, William, ex Grangepans, tailor, d. 1698 in Darien, reg. 1707. (CC8.8.83)

Kirk, Thomas, teacher in Rochester, New York, reg. 1893. (SC70.1.317)

Kirkpatrick, John, soldier, d. 1699 in Darien, reg. 1707. (CC8.8.83)

Kirwood, John, in Chicago, reg. 1872. (SC70.1.160)

Kitts, Isabella, in New York, reg. 1894.   (SC70.1.329)

Knolls, George, ex Bo'ness, sailor, d. 1698 in Darien,
     reg. 1707.   (CC8.8.83)

Knox, John, in Fishkill, New York, reg. 1852.   (SC70.1.77)

Knubley, Simon, in Jamaica, d. 26 Sep. 1836, reg. 1837.
     (SC70.1.55)(C1783)

Kretts, Henrick, trumpeter, d. 1698 in Darien, reg. 1707.
     (CC8.8.83)

Kretts, Paul, trumpeter, d. 1698 in Darien, reg. 1707.
     (CC8.8.83)

Kyd, William, in Montreal, reg. 1865.   (SC70.1.127)

Ladd, Alexander Morrison, in Oregon, reg. 1893. (SC70.1.323)

Laidlaw, Christian, wid of Francis Stewart, in Baltimore,
    Maryland, d. Oct. 1847, reg. 1862. (SC70.1.112)

Laidlaw, William, in Halifax, Nova Scotia, d. 7 Nov. 1827,
    reg. 1862. (SC70.1.111)(H1217)

Laing, Alexander Morrison, physician & surgeon in Kingston,
    Jamaica, reg. 1894. (SC70.1.330)

Laing, George, in Hamilton, Canada, reg. 1872. (SC70.1.157)

Laing, James, in Jamaica, d. 15 Dec. 1827, reg. 1845.
    (SC70.1.66)(E49)

Laing, John, planter in St Croix, d. 24 Aug. 1851, reg.
    1852. (SC70.1.74)(E2840)

Laing, William, in Freehold, Monmouth Co, New Jersey,
    d. 25 May 1738, reg. 1739. (CC8.8.101)

Lambie, Elisabeth Dundas, in Jamaica, d. 19 Dec. 1821.
    (D145)

Lamond, John, ex Fife, sailor, d. 1698 in Darien, reg.
    1707. (CC8.8.83)

Lamont, Boyden, planter in Trinidad, d. 31 Aug. 1837, reg.
    1838. (SC70.1.57)(C2015)   .

Lamont, Fletcher, in St Louis, USA, reg. 1875. (SC70.1.172)

Lamont of Benmore, John, planter in Trinidad, d. 21 Nov.
    1850, reg. 1851. (SC70.1.70)(E2611)

Landreth, Katherine, wid of Richard Landreth, in Grenada,
    reg. 1848. (SC70.1.68)

Langwill, Jessie, in Ingraham, Clinton Co, New York, reg.
    1899. (SC70.1.385)

Laporete, Joseph Polyxene, wid of Jean Baptiste Aquart,
in St Lucia, d. 7 Nov. 1837, reg. 1840.   (D1303)
(SC70.1.58)

Latta, James Douglas, in Duval, Texas, reg. 1896.
(SC70.1.351)

Lauder, Christian, in Jamaica, reg. 10 Sep. 1802.
(CC8.8.133)

Lauder, George, in Jamaica, reg. 10 Sep.1802.   (CC8.8.133)

Lauder, Mary, in Richmond Co, Georgia, reg. 12 Dec. 1797.
(CC8.8.130)

Lauder, Robert Seaton, in Jamaica, reg. 10 Sep. 1802.
(CC8.8.133)

Lauder, William, in Jamaica, reg. 10 Sep. 1802.
(CC8.8.133)

Laughton, Patrick, ex Orkney, gunner, d. 1698 in Darien,
reg. 1707.   (CC8.8.83)

Laurenson, Peter, at Lake Illinois, USA, reg. 1866.
(SC70.1.131)

Laurent, Arndee, merchant in Belize, reg. 1873.
(SC70.1.161)

Laurie, Archibald, merchant in Quebec, reg. 1886.
(SC70.1.246)

Laurie, Francis, merchant in Quebec, reg. 1886.
(SC70.1.246)

Lauson, William, ex Edinburgh, soldier, d. 1699 in Darien,
reg. 1707.   (CC8.8.83)

Law, William, ex Kirkcaldy, mariner, d. 1698 in Darien,
reg. 1707.   (CC8.8.83)

Law, William, physician in Belize, reg. 1878.   (SC70.1.192)

Lawrence, Sarah Jane, in Long Island, New York, reg. 1893.
    (SC70.1.318)

Lawrie, John, tailor in Oakville, Lake Ontario, Canada
    West, d. 23 Oct. 1855, reg. 1856.   (SC70.1.91)(H86)

Lawrie, Robert, in St George, St Vincent, d. 1770, reg.
    8 Jan. 1782.   (CC8.8.125)

Lawson, Isabella, in the West Indies, reg. 1881.
    (SC70.1.211)

Lawson, Robert, merchant in Virginia, d. Oct. 1787 in
    Glasgow, reg. 11 Jan. 1788.   (CC9.7.73)

Learmonth, Charles, ex Edinburgh, merchant, d. 1699 in
    Darien, reg. 1744.   (CC8.8.109)

Ledingham, John, in St John, Newfoundland, reg. 1898.
    (SC70.1.366)

Lees, Jane, in Hamilton, Canada, reg. 1891.   (SC70.1.296)

Lees, John, ex Edinburgh, gardener in New York, reg. 1894.
    (SC70.1.333)

Legg, John, merchant in Savanna la Mar, Jamaica, reg. 1776.
    (CC8.8.123)

Leiper, John, ex Drumboy, clergyman in Brandon, Manitoba,
    reg. 1887.   (SC70.1.259)

Leitch, George, in New Providence, reg. 1811.
    (CC8.8.138)(SC70.1.4)(B947)

Leith, Alexander, merchant in Philadelphia, reg. 17 July
    1750.   (CC8.8.113)

Leith, David, in Hanover, Jamaica, d. 5 Sep. 1841, reg. 1843.
    (SC70.1.63)(D1663)

Leith, John, in Kingston, Jamaica, reg. 4 Aug. 1800.
    (CC8.8.131)

Leitch, William, clergyman & academic, Principal of
    Queen's College, Kingston, Ontario, d. 9 May 1864,
    reg. 1864.   (SC70.1.123)(G3689)

Leslie, John Alexander, in Toronto, reg. 1889.   (SC70.1.279)

Leslie, Robert, inSanta Cruz, California, reg. 1890.
    (SC70.1.280)

Levy, Julius Emil, in New York, reg. 1899.   (SC70.1.380)

Lewis, John, blacksmith in StKitts, d. Jan. 1837, reg.
    1838.   (SC70.1.56)(C1936)

Liddal, Thomas Young, merchant in Belize, d. 2 Sep. 1844,
    reg. 1850.   (SC70.1.70)(E2225)

Liddell, John, clerk, d. 1699 in Darien,reg. 1708.
    (CC8.8.84)

Lighton, Patrick, ex Burntisland, seaman, d. 1699 in
    Darien, reg. 1707.   (CC8.8.83)

Linton, David, physician in St George, Grenada, d. in Ayr,
    reg. July 1809.   (CC9.7.80)

Liston, John, in Fishkill, New York, reg. 1852.
    (SC70.1.77)

Liston, Robert Henry, banker in Montreal, d. 29 June 1841,
    reg. 1842.   (SC70.1.62)(D1595)

Liston, Robert Ramage, in Maryland,d. 6 Jan. 1825, reg.
    30 June 1825.   (CC8.8.150)

Litster, Hugh, ex Fife, sailor, d. 1699 in Darien, reg.
    1708.   (CC8.8.84)

Littledale, Johnson, in Chicago, reg. 1863.   (SC70.1.221)

Livingston, Archibald Charles, in Jacksonville, USA, reg.
    1879.   (SC70.1.193)

Livingston, William Hardie, in Jersey City, reg. 1892.
    (SC70.1.314)

Loch, William, in Westmoreland, Jamaica, reg. 1815.
    (SC70.1.14)

Lockhart, Alexander, veterinary surgeon in New York, reg.
    1899.   (SC70.1.377)

Lockhart John, ex Prestonpans, sailor, d. 1699 in Darien,
    reg. 1707.   (CC8.8.83)

Lockie, Thomas Oman, in Toronto, reg. 1868.   (SC70.1.138)

Logan, Jean, wid of Alexander Buchanan, in Newport,
    St Mary's, Jamaica, d. Glasgow, reg. 13 Dec. 1823.
    (CC9.7.81)

Logan, W E, in Canada, reg. 1875.   (SC70.1.175)

Loggat, John, shipmaster in Philadelphia, reg. 15 June
    1785.   (CC8.8.126)

Logie, James, in Saurie's Island, Columbia, Oregon,
    d. Apr. 1854, reg. 1855.   (SC70.1.88)(F2126)

Lorimer, Harry James, in California, reg. 1895.
    (SC70.1.339)

Lorne, Peter, ex the Netherlands, cooper, d. 1698 in
    Darien, reg. 1707.   (CC8.8.83)

Lothian, Abraham, ex Renfrew, soldier, d. 1699 in
    Darien, reg. 1707.   (CC8.8.83)

Lothian, Patrick, mariner in New York, d. 23 May 1793,
    reg. 24 Dec. 1824.   (CC8.8.150)

Loudon, John, railway guard in Canada, d. 3 July 1857,
    reg. 1858.   (SC70.1.96)(H377)

Love, Christopher, ex Ayr, cooper, d. 1699 in Darien,
    reg. 1708.   (CC8.8.84)

Low, Grace Shaw, in Montreal, reg. 1882.   (SC70.1.216)

Low, William, ex Kirkcaldy, mariner, d. 1698 in Darien, reg. 1707. (CC8.8.83)

Low, William David, in Burton's Creek, Lynchburg, Virginia, reg. 1881. (SC70.1.211)

Lowndee, Henry, in Wallens, Jamaica, d. 24 May 1854, reg. 1855. (SC70.1.88)(E4424)

Lusk, John, exGreenock, in New York, reg. 1889. (SC70.1.276)

Lussan, Julien, in St George, Grenada, d. 24 Aug. 1826, reg. 1827. (SC70.1.37)(B1055)

Luttens, Herman, mariner, d. 1698 in Darien, reg. 1707. (CC8.8.83)

Lyall, James Mitchell, mason in Boston, reg. 1874. (SC70.1.167)

Lyall, William David, in Boston, reg. 1891. (SC70.1.291)

Lyell, John, farmer in San Saba, Texas, reg. 1898. (SC70.1.367)

Lyle, James, merchant in Virginia, d. 18 Feb. 1813 in Strathblane, reg. 29 Mar. 1813. (CC9.7.81)

Lyle, John, merchant in Nevis, d. Greenock, reg. 9 Feb. 1791. (CC9.7.74)

Lyon, Henry, sailor, d. 1699 in Darien, reg. 1707. (CC8.8.83)

Lyon, Robert, merchant in Tobago, d. 1786, reg. 7 May 1822. (CC8.8.148)

Lyster, Robina Alison, in Chicago, reg. 1888. (SC70.1.266)

Main, Helen, in Truro, Nova Scotia, reg. 1886. (SC70.1.251)

Maitland, John, d. 16 Jan. 1839 in Upper Canada. (D1319)

Maitland, William, ex Stirlingshire, sailor, d. 1698 in
Darien, reg. 1707. (CC8.8.83)

Maitland, William, ex Linlithgow, sailor, d. 1698 in Darien,
reg. 1707. (CC8.8.83)

Malcolm, Hugh, in Jamaica, d. Glasgow. reg 1795.
(CC9.7.75)

Malcolm, John, in Sedalia, reg. 1888. (SC70.1.269)

Malcolm, Quintin, ex Maybole, merchant in New England,
reg. 4 May 1752. (CC8.8.114)

Malloch, Edward, in Ottawa, reg. 1872. (SC70.1.157)

Malloch, James, in Montreal, reg. 1898. (SC70.1.369)

Malloch, John, ex Kirkcaldy, skipper, d. 1698 in Darien,
reg. 1709. (CC8.8.84)

Malloch, William, in Colorado Springs, reg. 1896.
(SC70.1.352)

Mansur, Alvah, in St Louis, Missouri, reg. 1898.
(SC70.1.367)

Marks, Dan, in Richmond, Virginia, d. 14 Apr. 1855, reg.
1857. (SC70.1.94)(H250)

Mornoch, John, in Cornwall, Jamaica, reg. 1818. (SC70.1.17)

Marjoribanks, Joseph, ex Edinburgh, sailor, d. 1698 in Darien,
reg. 1707. (CC8.8.83)

Marsh, Alex Pomeroy, in Chicago, reg. 1897. (SC70.1.360)

Marshall, William, ex Glasgow, merchant in Tobago, reg.
22 Apr. 1790. (CC8.8.128)

Marshall, William, ex Falkirk, merchant in Jamaica, reg.
10 Oct. 1796.   (CC8.8.130)

Martin, Alex, mariner in Toronto, reg. 1882.   (SC70.1.217)

Martin, Catherine, in Milwaukee, Wisconsin, reg. 1899.
(SC70.1.385)

Martin, Grizel, in Janefield, America, d. 1770.   reg.
22 Feb. 1777.   (CC8.8.124)

Martin, James, ex Linlithgow, sailor, d. 1699 in Darien,
reg. 1707.   (CC8.8.83)

Martin, Margaret, w of Robert Reid stonemason, in Montreal,
reg. 1884.   (SC70.1.233)

Martin, Rachel, sicknurse in Jamaica, d. 15 Nov. 1844.
(E287)

Martin, Robert, mason in Ohio, reg. 1894.   (SC70.1.332)

Mason, Alex, ex Hopeman, mason in St Vincent, d. 1820, reg.
1822.   (SC70.1.27)(CC8.8.148)

Mason, Janet, w of Robert Copley laborer, in New York,
d. 27 Nov. 1850, reg 1854.   (SC70.1.83)(F1851)

Mason, John, ex Burntisland, mariner, d. 1698 in Darien,
reg. 1707.   (CC8.8.83)

Mason, William, in New York, d. 14 Aug. 1849, reg. 1854.
(SC70.1.83)(F1856)

Masterton, Alex, ex Linlithgow, mariner, d. 1698 in Darien,
reg. 1723.   (CC8.8.89)

Masterton, David, in Baltimore, America, d. 10 Nov. 1833.
reg. 1837.   (SC70.1.55)(D991)

Mather, Arthur Gilmour, in Nashville, Tennessee, reg. 1896.
(SC70.1.346)

Mather, Edward Edmund, in Philadelphia, reg. 1899.
(SC70.1.376)

Matheson, John McLeod, silk merchant in New York, reg. 1895.
    (SC70.1.341)

Mathie, Thomas, sailor, d. 1699 in Darien, reg. 1707.
    (CC8.8.83)

Meiblo, James, ex Dysart, d. 1698 in Darien, reg. 1707.
    (CC8.8.83)

Meik, William, ex Bo'ness, sailor, d. 1699 in Darien, reg. 1707.
    (CC8.8.83)

Meiklejohn, Thomas, ex Queensferry, cook, d. 1700 in Darien,
    reg. 1712.   (CC8.8.85)

Mein, Robert, in Brooklyn, reg. 1888.   (SC70.1.265)

Melville, John, ex Kinghorn, sailor, d. 1699 in Darien,
    reg. 1707.   (CC8.8.83)

Melvin, John, in Montreal, reg. 1889.   (SC70.1.279)

Melville, John, in Kensington, Walsh County, Dakota, reg.
    1886.   (SC70.1.254)

Menzies, John, ex Edinburgh, merchant in Jamaica, d. 1768,
    reg. 21 Feb. 1769.   (CC8.8.121)

Menzies, Ninian, merchant in Richmond, Virginia and Eustatia,
    d. 1780, reg. 14 FEb. 1799.   (CC8.8.131)

Mercer, Joana Neilson, in Franklin, Oneida County, Idaho,
    reg. 1897.   (SC70.1.361)

Merchiston, Robert, ex Fife, surgeon, d. 1698 in Darien,
    reg. 1707.   (CC8.8.83)

Merston, John, soldier, d. 1699 in Darien, reg. 1707.
    (CC8.8.83)

Methven, Charles Caithness, ex Dundee, agent in Jamaica,
    d. 19 Apr. 1845, reg. 1853.   (SC70.1.80)(F1710)

Mever, Christopher, in United States, reg. 1889.   (SC70.1.274)

Middlemiss, James, in St Vincent, d. 15 Nov 1823, reg. 1831.
(SC70.1.45)(D304)

Miggleston, Thomas, ex Inverkeithing, sailor, d. 1699 in
DArien, reg. 1707. (CC8.8.83)

Mill, John, ex Aberlady, surgeon, d. 1699 in Darien, reg.
1708. (CC8.8.84)

Mill, William, ex Haddington, mariner, d. 1698 in Darien, reg.
1707. (CC8.8.83)

Miller, Agnes Janet, in Columbus County, Colorado, Texas,
reg. 1868. (SC70.1.141)

Miller, Alex, engineer in Montreal, d. 24 Feb. 1850 in North
Hero Island, Lake Champian, New York, reg. 1852.
(SC70.1.76)(F1507)

Miller, Daniel, baker in St Lucia, reg. 22 Jan. 1783.
(CC8.8.126)

Miller, Daniel, ex Kirkcaldy, sailor, d. 1698 in Darien, reg.
1707. (CC8.8.83)

Miller, Frederick George, clerk in Iowa, reg. 1882.
(SC70.1.218)

Miller, George, in Strawberry Hill, Long Island, Bahamas,
reg. 17 Aug. 1798. (CC8.8.131)

Miller, James, in New Providence, Bahamas, reg. 29 Mar. 1799.
(CC8.8.131)

Miller, James, in Harmony Hall, Jamaica, d. 4 Aug. 1836,
reg. 1837. (SC70.1.54)(D959)

Miller, James Broom, in Hanover, Ontario, reg. 1881.
(SC70.1.205)

Meikle, Isabella, in Chesley, Bruce County, Canada, reg. 1892.
(SC70.1.314)

Miller, John, ex Auchtertool, sailor, d. 1698 in Darien,
reg. 1707. (CC8.8.83)

Miller, John, in Gettysburg, USA, reg. 1868. (SC70.1.141)

Miller, Malcolm, sailor, d. 1698 in Darien, reg. 1707. (SC8.8.83)

Miller, Margaret, wid of Walter Miller merchant, in Jamaica, d. 18 Dec. 1847 in Granton, reg. 1852. (SC70.1.77) (F1550)

Miller, Mary, in St Louis, USA, reg. 1893. (SC70.1.325)

Miller, Robert, in Jamaica, d. 1810 in Glasgow, reg. 16 Jan. 1821. (CC9.7.81)

Miller, Thomas, merchant in Charleston, South Carolina, d. 1823 in Glasgow, reg. 17 Apr. 1823. (CC9.7.81)

Miller, William, ships carpenter in Wilmington, North Carolina, reg. 19 Oct. 1781. (CC8.8.125)

Miller, William, in Mamasonack, USA, reg. 1871. (SC70.1.153)

Milligan, William, in Mobile, d. 3 Apr. 1844, reg. 1845. (SC70.1.66)(F186)

Milne, Alexander, in Stanford, Connecticut, reg. 1989. (SC70.1.372)

Milne, Alexander Panton, in Palmyra, New York, reg. 1898. (SC70.1.370)

Milne, Jessie, in Winnipeg, reg. 1884. (SC70.1.230)

Milne, John Radcliffe, in Honduras, reg. 1827. (SC70.1.355)

Milne, William, customs officer in Old Harbor, Jamaica, d. 7 May 1850, reg. 1850. (SC70.1.78)(F1601)

Milroy, David, surgeon in Bermuda, reg. 1865. (SC70.1.126)

Mitchell, Alexander, in St Andrews, Jamaica, reg. 11 Jul. 1799. (CC8.8.131)

Mitchell, David, in Yamhill County, Oregon, reg. 1874.
(SC70.1.168)

Mitchell, Donald, in Blue Canyon, California, reg. 1889.
(SC70.1.276)

Mitchell, George Abercromby, in St Patrick, Grenada, d.
27 Jul. 1861 in Southampton, reg. 1862. (SC70.1.114)
(H1344)

Mitchell, James, ex Bo'ness, mariner, d. 1699 in Darien,
reg. 1707. (CC8.8.83)

Mitchell, James McNair, in Newfoundland, reg. 1894.
(SC70.1.329)

Mitchell, John, in Jamaica, reg. 1824. (SC70.1.32)

Mitchell, John, shipmaster in St John's, Newfoundland, reg.
1879. (SC70.1.192)

Mitchell, Margaret, in Argenteuil, Canada, d. 25 Oct. 1841,
reg. 1843. (SC70.1.63)

Mitchell, Walter, ex Alloway, sailor, d. 1698 in Darien,
reg. 1707. (CC8.8.83)

Moffat, James, ex Linlithgow, sailor, d. 1699 in Darien,
reg. 1707. (CC8.8.83)

Moncrieff, Archibald, merchant in Maryland, d. 6 Jan. 1803.
reg. 30 Nov. 1818. (CC8.8.144)

Moncrieff, David, soldier, d. 1699 in Darien, reg. 1707.
(CC8.8.83)

Moncrieff, George, carpenter, d. 1699 in Darien, reg. 1707.
(CC8.8.83)

Monro, Hugh, overseer, d. 1698 in Darien, reg. 1707.
(CC8.8.83)

Monteith, Thomas Loghlan, in Canadaiglia, New York, reg. 1872.
(SC70.1.159)

Montgomerie, Hugh, ex Port Glasgow, in Trinidad, reg. 1825. (SC70.1.32)

Montgomerie, Robert, in St Thomas, reg. 1824. (SC70.1.31)

Montgomery, Charles, in Jamaica, d. Feb. 1804. reg. 9 Oct. 1805. (CC8.8.136)

Montain, Joannes, ex Leith, sailor, d. 1698 in Darien, reg. 1707. (CC8.8.83)

Montignani, John Oswald, in Albany, New York, reg. 1896. (SC70.1.354)

Moodie, Jean, wid of Dr William Keith, in Charleston, South Carolina, reg. 18 May 1799. (CC8.8.131)

Moore, John Mitchell, in Jamaica, d. Jan. 1794, reg. 25 May 1794. (CC8.8.129)

Morgan, John, ex Leven, sailor, d. 1698 in Darien, reg. 1707. (CC8.8.83)

Morgan, Robert, in Colorado, reg. 1896. (SC70.1.354)

Moriseite, John, ex Burntisland, sailor, d. 1698 in Darien, reg. 1707. (CC8.8.83)

Morison, Jemima, ex Edinburgh, in Charleston, South Carolina, reg. 2 Jun. 1804. (CC8.8.135)

Morison, John, ex Aberdeenshire, merchant in Antigua, d. Dumfries, reg. 1770. (CC5.6.15)

Morison, John, in Real del Monte, Mexico, d. 16 Jul. 1853, reg. 1856. (SC70.1.92)(H184)

Morison, Thomas, in Port au Prince, Haiti, reg. 1876. (SC70.1.176)

Morison, William Gray, in Elgin, Beauharnois, Quebec, reg. 1884. (SC70.1.235)

Morris, Alexander, in Toronto, reg. 1890. (SC70.1.284)

Morris, David, in America, d. 1819, reg. 6 Feb. 1828.
(CC8.8.152)

Morrison, Christopher, ex Greenock, sailor, d. 1699 in Darien,
reg. 1707. (CC8.8.83)

Morrison, Eliza Finch, in Antigua, reg. 1867. (SC70.1.136)

Morrison, Mary, in Virginia, d. 11 Jun. 1829 in Edinburgh.
(C237)

Morrison, William, planter in Jamaica, reg. 1854. (SC70.1.8)
(E3965)

Morrison, William, in Fail River, Bristol, Massachusetts,
reg. 1889. (SC70.1.276)

Morton, Margaret, in Chicago, reg. 1872. (SC70.1.159)

Mott, John Prescott, in Dartmouth, Nova Scotia, reg. 1897.
(SC70.1.358)

Motton, Susan, in Port Hope, Canada, reg. 1885. (SC70.1.243)

Moultrie, Walter, ex Markinch, sailor, d. 1698 in Darien, reg.
1707. (CC8.8.83)

Mowat, John, in St Vincent, d. 16 Nov. 1843 in Edinburgh.
(F8)

Mowbray, Richard, in Ottawa, d. 18 Sep. 1858. reg. 1861.
(SC70.1.109)(H1069)

Moyes, James, ex Kinghorn, cooper, d. 1698 in Darien, reg.
1707. (CC8.8.83)

Mudie, Alexander, physician in Jamaica, d. 17 FEb. 1844 in
Edinburgh. (E187)

Muir, Alexander, ex Auchtermuchty, sailor, d. 1699 in Darien,
reg. 1707. (CC8.8.83)

Muir, Augusta, in St John's, Newfoundland, reg. 1878.
(SC70.1.191)

Muir, Elizabeth, in Rescott, Ontario, reg. 1891.   (SC70.1.292)

Muir, James, timber merchant in New Brunswick, reg. 1846.
     (SC70.1.66)

Muir, James, merchant in Liverpool, d. 22 Mar. 1850 in Jamaica,
     reg. 1850.   (SC70.1.71)(E2430)

Muir, John, physician and surgeon in Trelawney, Jamaica, d.
     21 Nov. 1816, reg. 1817.   (CC8.8.143)(SC70.1.16)

Muir, John, merchant in Kingston, Jamaica, d. 19 Mar. 1849,
     reg. 1852.   (SC70.1.74)(E2879)

Muir, William, ex Edinburgh, sailor, d. 1698 in Darien,
     reg. 1707.   (CC8.8.83)

Muir William, ex Edinburgh, in La Plata, Missouri, reg. 1889.
     (SC70.1.277)

Munn, Archibald, in Newfoundland, reg. 1877.   (SC70.1.186)

Munn Duncan, master mariner in Newfoundland, d. 1 Jun. 1855,
     reg. 1856.   (SC70.1.91)(H89)

Munro, Colin, planter in St Thomas in the East Middlesex,
     Jamaica, d. 1800, reg. 18 Jul. 1810.   (CC8.8.136)

Munro, John, in Grenada and Trinidad, d. 22 Jun. 1831.
     (C743)

Munro, John, ex Glasgow, ironmoulder in New York, reg. 1884.
     (SC70.1.238)

Munro, Margaret Arnott, in Wallace, Nova Scotia, reg. 1895.
     (SC70.1.345)

Munro, Moses, in St John's, Newfoundland, reg. 1897.
     (SC70.1.362)

Munro, Robert, in Jamaica, d. Feb. 1829.   reg. 1831.
     (SC70.1.44)(C266)

Murdoch, David Ritchie, commission agent in Montreal, reg.
     1895.   (SC70.1.337)

Murdoch, John, in America, d. 1844, reg. 1854.   (SC70.1.83)
    (F1854)

Mure, James, in California, reg. 1892.   (SC70.1.314)

Muriel, Ygnacio, in San Luis Potosi, Mexico, d. 25 May 1859.
    reg. 1861.   (SC70.1.107)(G2061)

Murray, Alexander, in Cumberland County, Providence, Rhode
    Island, reg. 1880.   (SC70.1.203)

Murray, Andrew, in St David, Jamaica, reg. 1844.   (SC70.1.66)

Murray, Alexander McGrigor, in Joppa, Maryland, d. 25 Sep. 1856,
    reg. 1863.   (SC70.1.118)(H1522)

Murray, Gabriel, merchant in Augusta, Georgia, d. 3 Jan. 1832,
    reg. 1832.   (SC70.1.47)(D368)

Murray, James, in Liberty, St Louis, d. 9 Nov. 1848.   reg.
    1850.   (SC70.1.70)(F1118)

Murray, Jean, in Charleston, South Carolina and Jamaica, d.
    1783, reg. 8 Jul. 1796.   (CC8.8.130)

Murray, Margaret, in Milwaukee, reg. 1897.   (SC70.1.364)

Murray, Sarah, ex Middleton, Midlothian, in New York, reg.
    1886.   (SC70.1.249)

Murray, William Cannon, merchant in Charleston, America,
    d. 29 May 1856, reg. 1856.   (SC70.1.92)(G333)

Muter, John, ex Kirkcudbright, customs searcher in St Lucia,
    d. Feb. 1815, reg. 1816.   (CC8.8.142)(SC70.1.14)

McAdam, Alexander, in Cook County, Illinois, reg. 1887.
    (SC70.1.256)

McAllister, Hector, merchant in New Providence, Bahamas, d.
    22 Aug. 1788, reg. 1866.   (SC70.1.131)

McArthur, Helen, in St Vincent, d. 17 Feb. 1838.   (C1893)

McArthur, Isabella, in Chesley, Bruce County, Canada, reg. 1892.   (SC70.1.314)

McArthur, John, surgeon in Grenada, reg. 1834.   (SC70.1.50)

McAulay, Robert, ex Glasgow, servant, d. 1699 in Darien, reg. 1707.   (CC8.8.83)

McCall, John, in Tobago, reg. 1886.   (SC70.1.198)

McCallum, M, in New York, reg. 1876.   (SC70.1.180)

McCallum, Margaret, ex Glasgow, in Washington, DC, reg. 1888. (SC70.1.266)

McCallum, Neil, in Hanover, Jamaica, d. 1835, reg. 1836. (C1523)

McCallum, Robert, in Minnesota, reg. 1876.   (SC70.1.176)

McCandlish, Grizel, in Janefield, America, d. 1770, reg. 22 Feb. 1777.   (CC8.8.124)

McCarter, James, in Willard City, Utah, reg. 1883. (SC70.1.221)

MacCartney, James, merchant in Mexico, d. 22 Aug. 1839 in Edinburgh, reg. 1839.   (SC70.1.58)

McCaskie, James, in St Domingo, d. 7 Jun. 1798, reg. 6 Mar. 1799.   (CC8.8.131)

McCaw, James, surgeon in Virginia, reg. 2 Jun. 1791. (CC8.8.129)

McClelland, John, in San Salvador, Guatamala, d. Aug. 1832, reg. 1835.   (SC70.1.52)(D768)

McClenaghan, Andrew Thomson, in St Vincent, reg. 1881. (SC70.1.211)

McColl, Hugh, in New York, reg. 1876.   (SC70.1.178)

McColm, Quintin, ex Maybole, merchant in New England, d. 3 Aug. 1746, reg. 1752.   (CC8.8.114)

Maconachie, William, clergyman in Portobacco, Maryland, reg. 21 Jan. 1743. (CC8.8.107)

McCormick, William, merchant in North Carolina, d. 16 Jan. 1815, reg. 28 Jun. 1821. (CC8.8.147)

McCracken, Patrick, in St Lucia, d. 14 Dec. 1839.   reg. 1841. (SC70.1.60)(D1429)

McCulloch, Anthony, in Queen Anne County, Maryland, d. 1770, reg. 30 Apr. 1773. (CC8.8.122)

Mc Culloch, Hugh, in Yonkers, Westchester County, USA, reg. 1888. (SC70.1.264)

McCulloch, John, ex Argyll, sailor, d. 1698 in Darien, reg. 1709. (CC8.8.84)

McCulloch, John, in Trinidad, Sugar Estate, Cuba, reg. 1888. (SC70.1.264)

McCulloch, Michael, physician in Montreal, reg. 1867. (SC70.1.137)

McCulloch, Thomas, in Rome, USA, reg. 1881. (SC70.1.211)

McCulloch, William, merchant in Vera Cruz, d. Aug. 1848, reg. 1850. (SC70.1.70)(F1020)

McDonald, Alexander, in Montreal, reg. 1860. (SC70.1.104)

McDonald, David, ex Lochbank, d. 1699 in Darien, reg. 1709. (CC8.8.84)

McDonald, Grace, in Acadia Mines, Colchester, Nova Scotia, reg. 1887. (SC70.1.259)

McDonald, John, merchant in Montreal, reg. 1891. (SC70.1.296)

McDonald, John, in Kingston, Jamaica, reg. 1899. (SC70.1.383)

McDonald, Laughlin, in Earlstown, Nova Scotia, reg. 1869. (SC70.1.145)

MacDonald, Mary, in St Louis, USA, reg. 1893.   (SC70.1.325)

MacDonald, Patrick, ex Perth, s of Patrick MacDonald, in
    Jamaica, reg. 29 Sep. 1772.   (CC8.8.122)

MacDonald, William, Lieutenant Governor in Fort Augusta, Jamaica,
    reg. 21 Dec. 1791.   (CC8.8.129)

McDougall, William, planter in St Catherine, Jamaica, d. 1804,
    reg. 14 Sep. 1807.   (CC8.8.137)

McDowall, James, in New York, d. in Dunfermline, reg. 1888.
    (SC70.1.266)

McDowell, Allen, in Parkhead, St Vincent, d. 16 Apr. 1837,
    reg. 1844.   (SC70.1.65)(E111)

McDowall, Daniel, in St Vincent, d. 19 May 1829, reg. 1831.
    (SC70.1.45)(C496)

McDuffie, Janet, ex Argyll, in Kingston, Jamaica, d. 1790,
    reg. 30 Jul. 1799.   (CC8.8.131)

McEachern, Archibald, merchant in Belize, reg. 1855.
    (SC70.1.87)

MacEachnie, Samuel, planter in Tobago, d. 27 Apr. 1840, reg.
    1841.   (SC70.1.60)(C2526)

McElroy, Janet, New York, reg. 1872.   (SC70.1.158)

McEwan, Alexander, carpenter in Grenada, d. 4 Aug 1841.
    reg. 1842.   (SC70.1.62)(C2911)

MacEwan, George William, ex Edinburgh, in Toronto, reg. 1881.
    (SC70.1.206)

McEwan, John, in Martinique, d. 1795, reg. 21 Apr. 1813.
    (CC8.8.139)

McEwan, Margaret, in Milwaukee, reg. 1897.   (SC70.1.364)

McEwan, Matthew Clark, in Chicago, reg. 1899.   (SC70.1.385)

McEwan, William, merchant in West Indies, d. 1776, reg.
    16 Jun. 1813.   (CC8.8.139)

McFadzean, James, draper in Roseau, Dominica, reg. 1868. (SC70.1.139)

McFarlane, John, physician in Jamaica, d 5 May 1862 in Edinburgh, reg. 1862. (SC70.1.114)(G2783)

McFarquhar, Colin, in St George, Barbados, reg. 1784. (CC8.8126)

McFie, John, ex Rothesay, piper, d. 1699 in Darien, reg. 1710, (CC8.8.84)

McGibbon, Peter, in Norfolk, Virginia, d. Jul. 1788 at sea, reg. 18 Apr. 1788. (CC9.7.73)

McGlashan, John Fergus, ex Kinghorn, in Canada, reg. 1882. (SC70.1.216)

McGowan, Mary, in Glenlyon, Dauphin, Manitoba, reg. 1899. (SC70.1.382)

McGregor, Daniel, ex Calton, sailor, d. 1699 in Darien, reg. 1707. (CC8.8.83)

McGregor of McGregor, John Atholl, d. 11 May 1851 in Tortula, reg. 1855. (SC70.1.88)(E2789)

McGregor, John, in Visalia, California, reg. 1876. (SC70.1.179)

McGregor, Neil, in Jamaica, reg. 19 Sep. 1798. (CC8.8.131)

McGregor, Patrick, merchant in St Thomas in the East Jamaica, reg. 16 Jun. 1823. (CC8.8.149)(SC70.1.28)

McGuire, Lauchlane McQuarry, ex Campbelltown, shipmaster in New York, d. Jan. 1783, reg. 20 May 1785.

McInnes, Andrew, in Charlotteville, Canada reg. 1891. (SC70.1.299)

McIntosh, Duncan, ex Edinburgh, merchant in Jamaica, reg. 18 May 1744. (CC8.8.108)

McIntosh, John, in Kakalau, Hawaii, d. in Mexico, reg. 1900.
(SC70.1.392)

McIntosh, Lachlan, ex Inverness, hairdresser in Hamilton, Canada West, d. 11 Aug 1854, reg. 1854. (SC70.1.85)(F1957)

McIntosh, William, in Tacoma, Washington, reg. 1892.
(SC70.1.311)

McIntyre, Catherine, in San Bernardino, California, reg. 1888.
(SC70.1.267)

McIvor, John, in Georgia and New York, reg. 1824. (SC70.1.31)

McJerrow, John, in Brooklyn, reg. 1898. (SC70.1.372)

Mackay, George, in Savanna Grande, Trinidad, d. 3 Sep. 1837, reg. 1838. (SC70.1.57)(C1984)

Mackay, George Grant, in Vancouver, reg. 1893. (SC70.1.319)

Mackay, James, physician and surgeon in St Thomas in the East Jamaica, reg. 1798. (CC8.8.131)

Mackay, Robert, watchman with the Pacific Railroad in Valligo, California, reg. 1881. (SC70.1.211)

McKean, Elizabeth, in Salt Lake City, reg. 1888.
(SC70.1.265)

MacKellar, Dugald, in St John's, Newfoundland, d. 6 Jan. 1847, reg. 1848. (SC70.1.68)(E1406)

McKendrick, Quentin K, in New York, reg. 1895. (SC70.1.334)

McKendrick, John, in Port Elgin, Ontario, reg. 1891.
(SC70.1.298)

McKendrick, William Ramsay, warehouseman in Chicago, reg. 1873.
(SC70.1.326)

McKenny, James, ex Carsedyke, carpenter, d. Apr 1700 in Darien, reg. 1707. (CC8.8.83)

McKenzie, Alexander, soldier, d. 1699 in West Indies, reg. 1707. (CC8.8.83)

McKenzie, Alexander, ex Edinburgh, tailor in Charleston, North America, d. 1793, reg. 5 Dec. 1811. (CC8.8.138)

Mackenzie, Colin Nicolson, surgeon in America, reg. 1872. (SC70.1.158)

MacKenzie, David, ex Inverness, officer in Royal American Regiment, reg. 11 Jan. 1776. (CC8.8.123)

Mackenzie, Douglas, in Snell Hall Estate, Grenada, d. 11 Jul. 1854. reg. 1855. (SC70.1.89)(F2147)

McKenzie, George, ex Edinburgh, merchant in Barbados, reg. 15 Jun. 1733. (CC8.8.95)

McKenzie, Hector, surgeon, d. 12 Aug 1699 in America, reg. 1707. (CC8.8.83)

Mackenzie, Joanna, in Ashtkosh, Wisconsin, reg. 1882. (SC70.1.214)

McKenzie, John, gunner, d. 1698 in Darien, reg. 1707. (CC8.8.83)

MacKenzie, John, in Jamaica, reg. 9 Feb. 1785. (CC8.8.126)

McKenzie, John, in Philadelphia, reg. 1809. (SC70.1.1)

Mackenzie, John, ex Ross-shire, in San Francisco, reg. 1886. (SC70.1.253)

McKenzie, Kenneth, in Georgia, reg. 1868. (SC70.1.137)

McKenzie, Margaret, in St Catherine, Middlesex, Jamaica, d. 1800, reg. 11 Feb. 1801. (CC8.8.132)

McKenzie, Murdo John, in Oneida, Canada, d. 18 Jul. 1848, reg. 1849. (SC70.1.69)(E1734)

Mackenzie, Patrick Mitchell, physician in Tobago, reg. 1875. (SC70.1.174)

McKerrall, William, in Dallas, Texas, reg. 1874.　(SC70.1.170)

Mackie, George, ex Fife, sailor, d. 1698 in Darien, reg. 1707.
　　(CC8.8.83)

Mackie, John Saddler, in Salem, Massachusetts, reg. 1874.
　　(SC70.1.168)

McKill, Robert, planter in Concordia, Tobago, d. 21 Nov. 1821
　　reg. 13 Apr. 1822.　(CC8.8.148)(SC70.1.26)

MacKindlay, Alexander, physician in Jamaica, d. Leith, reg.
　　3 Oct. 1774.　(CC8.8.123)

McKinna, John, ex Edinburgh, merchant in Jamaica, reg. 31 Jan.
　　1766.　(CC8.8.120)

McKinnel, John, shipmaster of "Fame of New York" in New York,
　　reg. 16 Jul. 1784.　(CC8.8.126)

McKinnell, Robert, in Pickering, Ontario, reg. 1894.
　　(SC70.1.329)

McKinnon, Isabella, in Portage la Prairie, Canada, reg. 1895.
　　(SC70.1.337)

McKnight, Thomas, in Hoboken, New Jersey, reg. 1900.
　　(SC70.1.386)

McLachlan, George, in British Columbia, reg. 1895.
　　(SC70.1.338)

McLachlane, John Alexander, in Yorkville County, Racine,
　　Wisconsin, d. 7 Nov. 1857, reg. 1860.　(SC70.1.104)
　　(H850)

McLaren, Alexander, in St Kitts, reg. 1868.　(SC70.1.140)

McLaren, M, in New York, reg. 1876.　(SC70.1.180)

McLarty, Charles, ex Campbelltown, physician in Jamaica,
　　d. 6 Sep. 1812, reg. 16 Sep. 1813.　(CC8.8.139)
　　(SC70.1.8)

McLaws, Jane, in Salt Lake City, reg. 1895.　(SC70.1.342)

McLean, Agnes, ex Edinburgh, in San Francisco, reg. 1887.
    (SC70.1.258)

McLean, Charles, in St Mary's, Middlesex, Jamaica, d. 1804.
    reg. 27 May 1823.   (CC8.8.149)

McLean, Donald, ex Argyll, planter and merchant in St Augustine,
    Florida, d. 1778, reg. 25 Jan. 1786.   (CC8.8.127)

McLean, Duncan, officer in 2nd West Indies Regiment, reg.
    1825.   (SC70.1.33)

McLean, Ewan, in New York, reg. 1877.   (SC70.1.181)

McLean, George Duncan, book-keeper in Jamaica, d. 31 Jan. 1859,
    reg. 1859.   (SC70.1.102)(H721)

McLean, Hugh, in Spanish Town, Jamaica, reg. 1846.   (SC70.1.66)

McLean, James, in St Mary's, Middlesex, Jamaica, d. 1804,
    reg. 27 May 1823.   (CC8.8.149)

MacLean, Murdoch, officer in West Indies Regiment, reg.
    6 Jan. 1797.   (CC8.8.130)

McLeay, Donald, in Portland, Oregon, reg. 1898.   (SC70.1.366)

Maclehose, Agnes, in Jamaica, d. 22 Oct. 1841 in Edinburgh,
    reg. (D1568)

Maclehose, James, attorney in Kingston, Jamaica, d. 16 Mar.
    1812, reg. 17 Jun. 1817.   (CC8.8.143)(SC70.1.16)

McLellan, James, merchant in Grenada, reg. 27 Feb. 1788.
    (CC8.8.127)

McLeod, Alexander, in Dominica, d. 179-, reg. 15 Jun. 1798.
    (CC8.8.131)

McLeod, Murdoch, in Brantford, Canada, reg. 1873.
    (SC70.1.164)

McMillan, Alexander, in Pittstown, Luzern, Pennsylvania,
    d. 4 Nov. 1859, reg. 1860.   (SC70.1.106)(H916)

McMillan, Neil, in Charlotte, StVincent, d. 26 Jun. 1842, reg. 1842. (SC70.1.62)(D1603)

McMurrich, John, in Toronto, reg. 1886. (SC70.1.250)

McNair, Hugh, ex Paisley, waiter in New Orleans, d. Feb. 1844, reg. 1852. (SC70.1.74)(F1382)

McNair, James, ex Paisley, baker in New Orleans, d. Aug. 1843, reg. 1852. (SC70.1.74)(F1381)

McNair, Robert, ex Glasgow, cooper, d. 1698 in Darien, reg. 1707. (CC8.8.83)

McNairne, Hannah, ex Newton Stewart, w of Hugh Peacock tailor, in America, reg. 2 Jul. 1785. (CC8.8.126)

McNally, John, ex Paisley, in New Orleans, reg. 1886. (SC70.1.251)

McNaught, Charles Henry, in Pennsylvania, reg. 1866. (SC70.1.132)

McNaught, David George, ex Edinburgh, in Montreal, reg. 1889. (SC70.1.280)

MacNee Jeannie, ex Glasgow, in Callegaute, Mexico, reg. 1990. (SC70.1.391)

McNeil, Hugh, merchant in Antigua, d. Ballantrae, reg. 1762. (CC9.7.64)

McNeill, John, in Paisley, Bruce County, Canada, reg. 1873. (SC70.1.161)

McNeil, John, druggist in St John's, Newfoundland, reg. 1898. (SC70.1.373)

McNeill, Malcolm, in Jamaica, reg. 20 Apr. 1785. (CC8.8.126)

McNeil, Neil, merchant and planter in Hanover, Jamaica, d. 1749 in Glasgow, reg. 1785. (CC9.7.60/73)

McNeill, Neill, mariner, d. 1699 in Darien, reg. 1707. (CC8.8.83)

McNeish, Thomas, in Benton Harbor, Michigan, reg. 1888. (SC70.1.266)

McNeran, Malcolm, in Philadelphia, d. 18 Mar. 1806, reg. 1842. (SC70.1.61)(D1548)

McNicol, John, in Kingston, Jamaica, reg. 9 Jan. 1816. (CC8.8.142)

MacNicol, John, in Ivanhoe, Florida, reg. 1894. (SC70.1.335)

McPherson, Andrew, surgeon in Tobago, reg. 1857. (SC70.1.96)

McPherson, Barbara, in Washington, USA, d. 10 May 1864, reg. 1865. (SC70.1.126)(H1885)

McPherson, Emma Jessie, in Montpelier, Tobago, reg. 1891. (SC70.1.296)

McPherson, John, in St Thomas in the East Jamaica, d. Aug. 1800, reg. 15 Dec. 1801. (CC8.8.132)

McPherson, John, in Jamaica, d. 19 Nov. 1838 in Loanhead. (C2416)

McPherson, John, in Boston, reg. 1873. (SC70.1.163)

McPherson, William, in Vere, Middlesex, Jamaica, d. 25 May 1798, reg. 20 Sep. 1820. (CC8.8.145)

McQueen, William, physician in Jamaica, reg. 21 Apr. 1804. (CC8.8.135)

McRae, John, in Lottery, Trelawney, Jamaica, d. 25 Oct. 1837, reg. 1838. (SC70.1.56)(D1067)

MacRitchie, Thomas Elder, in Kansas, reg. 1876. (SC70.1.176)

McRobbie, William, clergyman in Loudon, Canada, reg. 1894. (SC70.1.329)

McTavish, Hugh George, in Virginia, reg. 1873. (SC70.1.165)

McVicar, Archibald, overseer in Sixteen Mile Walk, Jamaica, reg. 3 Dec. 1763. (CC8.8.119)

McVicar, Marjory, in Kingston, Jamaica, d. 23 Oct. 1827, reg.
    28 May 1829.   (CC8.8.152)(68)

MvVittie, Grace Nisbet, in Utica, Michigan, reg. 1896.
    (SC70.1.348)

McWhannel, Thomas Douglas, in US Club, reg. 1877.   (SC70.1.183)

McWilliam, Helen, in Brant, Bruce County, Ontario, reg. 1887.
    (SC70.1.257)

McWilliam, John, planter in Grenada, d. 1 Aug. 1826, reg. 1827.
    (SC70.1.35)(B898)

Nairn, Mary, in Murraybay, Canada, d. 14 May 1821. (D3)

Nairne, Christian, da of Col John Nairne, in Lower Canada,
    d. 17 Jul. 1817, reg. 1820. (SC70.1.21)

Nairne, Christine, in Murraybay, Canada, d. 10 Apr. 1828,
    reg. 1829. (SC70.1.39)(C2)

Nairne, Jane Bowhill, in Michaux, Powhatan County, Virginia,
    reg. 1900. (SC70.1.393)

Naismith, William, ex Bo'ness, sailor, d. 1698 in Darien,
    reg. 1707. (CC8.8.83)

Nairsmith, John, ex Edinburgh, merchant in Virginia, d. 1747,
    reg. 9 Jul. 1752. (CC8.8.114)

Nay, John, in St Catherine, Canada, reg. 1875. (SC70.1.176)

Neil, Robert, Commissary General in Barbados, reg. 1853.
    (SC70.1.78)

Neil, Thomas, merchant in Trinidad, d. 25 Mar. 1843, reg. 1844.
    (SC70.1.66)(E242)

Neillands, Robert, gunner in Montreal, d. 3 Oct. 1840, reg.
    1843. (SC70.1.64)(D1768)

Neilson, Thomas, clerk, d. 1698 in Darien, reg. 1707.
    (C8.8.83)

Neilson, Thomas, merchant in Jamaica, d. Feb. 1800 in Glasgow,
    reg. 1 May 1800. (CC9.7.77)

Newbigging, David, in Bayham, London, Canada, d. Jul. 1853,
    reg. 1856. (SC70.1.92)(G376)

Newton, Ann, in Missouri, reg. 1898. (SC70.1.369)

Newton, Catherine, in Acomack, Virginia, reg. 17 Oct. 1788.
    (SC70.1.212)

Nicholson, Agnes Rewid, ex Edinburgh, in Washington, DC, reg.
    1882. (SC70.1.212)

Nicholson, Elizabeth Dickson, in Morton, Kingston, Ontario, reg. 1890. (SC70.1.289)

Nicholson, William, foreman in Boar Island, Bermuda, d. 2 Mar 1858, reg. 1858. (SC70.1.98)(H520)

Nicolson, John, in Newfoundland, d. 1829 in Edinburgh. (C92

Nicholson, Thomas, joiner in Clarendon, Jamaica, d. 10 Jul. 1822, reg. 8 Aug. 1826. (CC8.8.151)

Nimmo, Andrew, ex Airth, mariner, d. 1698 in Darien, reg. 1707. (CC8.8.83)

Nisbet, George, ex Edinburgh, in Jamaica, reg. 1895. (SC70.1.338)

Nisbet, Robert, merchant in Nevis and St Kitts, reg. 10 Dec. 1743. (CC8.8.108)

Niven, William, in Anaconda, Montana, reg. 1895. (SC70.1.345)

Niven, John Paterson, in Paterson, New Jersey, d. 16 Aug. 1840, reg. 1846. (SC70.1.66)(E602)

Nooney, Helen, in Illinois, reg. 1894. (SC70.1.334)

Norrie, Robert, ex Dalkeith, sailor, d. 1698 in Darien, reg. 1707. (CC8.8.83)

Norrie, George, laborer in Bromden, Manitoba, reg. 1883. (SC70.1.28)

Norrie, John Sanderson, in Toronto, reg. 1898. (SC70.1.368)

Norris, Henry Lee, physician in West Hoboken, Hudson County, New Jersey, reg. 1900. (SC70.1.391)

Norris, Marian Schaeffer, in New York, reg. 1890. (SC70.1.283)

Ochterlony, Patrick, in Calvert Co, Maryland, reg. 5 July 1758. (CC8.8.117)

Ogilvie, Alexander, in America, reg. 6 July 1790. (CC8.8.128)

Ogilvie, James, commission agent in New York, reg. 1837. (SC70.1.56)

Ogilvy, Henry, shipmaster in Charleston, South Carolina, d. 1779, reg. 27 May 1784. (CC8.8.126)

Ogilvy, John, overseer, d. 1699 in Darien, reg. 1707. (CC8.8.83)

Ogilvy, Katherine Gray, in Strongsville, Ohio, reg. 1880. (SC70.1.204)

Ogilvie, Thomas, ex Banff, merchant in St Kitts, reg. 5 Oct. 1774. (CC8.8.123)

Ogilvy, Weller Edington, in Ohio, reg. 1870. (SC70.1.149)

Old, John, merchant in Virginia, reg. 28 Oct. 1803. (CC8.8.134)

Oliphant, Ann Hay, in Colorado, reg. 1892. (SC70.1.306)

Oliphant, Margaret, in St Catherine, Middlesex, Jamaica, d. 1800, reg. 11 Feb. 1801. (CC8.8.132)

Oliphant, Jemima, ex Edinburgh, in Charleston, South Carolina, reg. 2 June 1804. (CC8.8.135)

Oliphant, John, ex Kirkcaldy, mariner, d. 1698 in Darien, reg. 1707. (CC8.8.83)

Oliphant, Laurence, ex Williamstown, mariner, d. 1698 in Darien, reg. 1707. (CC8.8.83)

Oliphant, Thomas, ex Shetland Islands, sailor, d. 1698 in Darien, reg. 1708. (CC8.8.84)

Ormiston, John Andrew, in America, reg. 1883. (SC70.1.223)

Orr, James, ex Ayr, merchant in Jamaica, d. 1750, reg. 11 Feb. 1758. (CC8.8.117)

Orr, John, engineer in Sherbrook, Canada, reg. 1886. (SC70.1.253)

Orrock, Alexander, ex Fife, sailor, d. 1698 in Darien, reg. 1707. (CC8.8.83)

Orrock, John, ex Kinghorn, sailor, d. 1698 in Darien, reg. 1707. (CC8.8.83)

Orrok, Fergus Edgar, in New York & Jersey City, reg. 1900. (SC70.1.394)

Osborn, William, in Content, St James, Jamaica, d. 18 Sep. 1850, reg. 1851. (SC70.1.72)(E2567)

Ouchterlony, Mary, in Kingston, Jamaica, d. 17 Dec. 1852, reg. 1853. (SC70.1.80)(E3507)

Oughterson, Arthur, merchant in Barbados, d. in Greenock, reg. 2 July 1817. (CC9.7.83)

Ovens, James, in Baltimore, reg. 1884. (SC70.1.229)

Owans, Thomas, sailor in Jamaica, d. 1740, reg. 22 Feb. 1777. (CC8.8.124)

Paine, George, in St Thomas in the East, Jamaica,
   reg. 1845.   (SC70.1.66)

Park, Patrick, ex Glasgow, merchant, d. 1698 in Darien,
   reg. 1707.   (CC8.8.83)

Parker, George, merchant in Hamilton, Ontario, d. 3 Sep.
   1860 in New York, reg. 1861.   (SC70.1.109)(G2304)

Parker, George, merchant in Hamilton, Canada, reg. 1876.
   (SC70.1.177)

Paterson, Alexander Baird, cabinet-maker in New York,
   reg. 1886.   (SC70.1.250)

Paterson, Elizabeth, in New York, d. 17 Jan. 1853,
   reg. 1857.   (SC70.1.94)(H292)

Paterson, Janet, ex Glasgow, in Montreal, reg. 1889.
   (SC70.1.285)

Paterson, John, clergyman in Chatham, Canada, reg. 1882.
   (SC70.1.213)

Patison, William, merchant in St Lucia, reg. 1848.
   (SC70.1.68)

Patrick, Jane, in New York, reg. 1891.   (SC70.1.298)

Patterson, James, merchant in Givara, Cuba, d. 7 June 1857,
   reg. 1860.   (SC70.1.105)(D1497)

Patterson, Livingston, in South Carolina, d. 1831, reg.
   1841.   (SC70.1.61)(D1497)

Patterson, Robert, farmer in Landsdowne, Upper Canada,
   d. 6 July 1854, reg. 1861.   (SC70.1.122)(H1726)

Patterson, Samuel, merchant in Charleston, South
   Carolina, d. 1838, reg. 1841.   (SC70.1.61)(D1491)

Patterson, Thomas, ex Edinburgh, cloth-merchant, d. 1813
   in Jamaica.   (F105)

Patterson, Jonas, ex Leith, carpenter, d. 1699 in Darien, reg. 1707. (CC8.8.83)

Pattison, William, merchant in Castries, St Lucia, d. 12 Feb. 1843, reg. 1848. (SC70.1.68)(E1599)

Patton, Henry, ex Bo'ness, mariner, d. 1698 in Darien, reg. 1707. (CC8.8.83)

Pattullo, David, merchant in New York, reg. 1870. (SC70.1.146)

Paul, George, in Panton, Jamaica, d. 29 Mar. 1834. (F242)

Paxton, John, ex Edinburgh, d. 4 Oct. 1861 in Louisville, USA, reg. 1862. (SC70.1.111)(G2485)

Peacock, Hannah, in America, reg. 2 July 1785. (CC8.8.126)

Pedden, James, ex Prestonpans, sailor, d. 1699 in Darien, reg. 1707. (CC8.8.83)

Peddie, Robert, physician in Antigua, d. 16 Nov. 1841, reg. 1860. (SC70.1.103)(G1592)

Penman, Robert Patterson, in Fort Wayne, Allan Co, Indiana, reg. 1899. (SC70.1.382)

Pennycook, Robert, in Westmoreland, Cornwall Co, Jamaica, d. 13 Sep. 1826, reg. 1 June 1827. (CC8.8.151)(B1001)

Peock, James, in St Vincent, d. 14 Dec. 1812, reg. 16 Sep. 1814. (CC8.8.140)(SC70.1.11)

Perry, Amelia, in Montreal, d. 21 Aug. 1827 in Edinburgh. (B1084)

Perry, Jane McLaws, in Salt Lake City, reg. 1895. (SC70.1.342)

Philip, Alexander Brockie, in Belize, reg. 1897. (SC70.1.360)

Philips, Robert, ex Leven, sailor, d. 1699 in Darien, reg. 1707. (CC8.8.83)

Philp, John, in Nashville, Iowa, reg. 1885. (SC70.1.242)

Pinch, John, in Bowmanville, Ontario, reg. 1892. (SC70.1.305)

Pinder, Margaret, in Barbados, reg. 1842. (SC70.1.62)

Pinkerton, Robert, ex Edinburgh, mariner, d. 1699 in Darien, reg. 1707. (CC8.8.83)

Pitcairn, David, merchant in Jamaica, d. Oct. 1730, reg. 28 Dec. 1733. (CC8.8.95)

Pitscottie, Colin, sailor, d. 1699 in Darien, reg. 1707. (CC8.8.83)

Plaine, James, ex Paris, merchant in Savanna, Georgia, d. Sep. 1798, reg. 23 Feb. 1807. (CC8.8.136)

Pollock, Allan, in Chelsea, Virginia, d. Jan. 1816, reg. 26 Jan. 1819. (CC8.8.145)(SC70.1.18)

Pollock, Elizabeth, in Osgoode, Carleton, Canada, reg. 1895. (SC70.1.337)

Pollock, M A, in Fredericksburg, reg. 1876. (SC70.1.179)

Pollock, Robert, merchant in Petersburg, North America, d. May 1811, reg. 17 June 1813. (CC8.8.139)(SC70.1.8)

Ponton, Archibald, baker in the Bahamas, d. 17 Sep. 1799, reg. 10 Aug. 1804. (CC8.8.135)

Porteous, Samuel, in Trinidad, reg. 1889. (SC70.1.277)

Porter, M A, in Fredericksburg, reg. 1876. (SC70.1.179)

Potter, James, in Kansas, reg. 1876. (SC70.1.180)

Pourie, Alexander, ex Edinburgh, sailor, d. 1698 in Darien, reg. 1707. (CC8.8.83)

Power, Edward, seaman, d. 1698 in Darien, reg. 1707. (CC8.8.83)

Pratt, Alexander, ex Edinburgh, in Hamilton, Bermuda, reg. 1888. (SC70.1.265)

Pratt, Thomas, ex Bo'nesss, sailor, d. 1698 in Darien, reg. 1708. (CC8.8.84)

Preston, James, in Rusk Co, Texas, reg. 1892. (SC70.1.309)

Pringle, Walter, merchant in St Kitts, d. 1760, reg. 13 Aug. 1776. (CC8.8.123)

Provan, Hugh, s of Hugh Provan of Auchinloch, in Isle of Wight, Virginia, d. in Govan, reg. 9 Jan. 1790. (CC10.5.12)

Pugh, Christina, in Camp Hall, Virginia, d. 30 Mar. 1864, reg. 1871. (SC70.1.21)(H1693)

Punton, William, merchant in Newfoundland, d. 15 Mar. 1845 in Aberdeen, reg. 1845. (SC70.1.66)(E501)

Purves, George, ex Dunbar, in Pine Bluff, Arkansas, reg. 1900. (SC70.1.388)

Purves, James, farmer in Lake Co, California, reg. 1888. (SC70.1.267)

Purves, John Archibald, in Toronto, reg. 1877. (SC70.1.183)

Purvis, Burridge, in Oakland, North America, d. 1 Sep. 1837, reg. 1864. (SC70.1.19)(G3655)

Purvis, John, in Warren, Mississippi, d. 19 Oct. 1850 in Edinburgh, reg. 1864. (SC70.1.122)(E3140)

Purvis, William, in Charleston, South Carolina, d. 23 Jan. 1842, reg. 1861. (SC70.1.107)(G2099)

Purvis, William, planter in Mississippi, reg. 1867. (SC70.1.136)

Queely, Dorothy, in St Kitts, reg. 10 Feb. 1777. (CC8.8.124)

Rae, George MacAuley, in Missouri, reg. 1877.
(SC70.1.186)

Rae, George MacAuley, in New York, reg. 1878.
(SC70.1.190)

Rae, William, merchant in Kingston, Jamaica, d. 7 May 1837,
reg. 1837. (SC70.1.55)(C1759)

Rae, William, in Montreal, reg. 1897. (SC70.1.356)

Railey, Jessie Johnston, in New Orleans, reg. 1899.
(SC70.1.383)

Rainy, William, in Jamaica, reg. 1847. (SC70.1.68)

Ramsay, David, in Charlottetown, Prince Edward Island,
reg. 1883. (SC70.1.227)

Ramsay, George, in St Vincent, reg. 29 July 1775.
(CC8.8.123)

Randall, Margaret, in Belleville, Canada, d. 13 Jan. 1844,
reg. 1846. (SC70.1.66)(F310)

Rankeiller, Thomas, ex Wemyss, sailor, d. 1699 in Darien,
reg. 1708. (CC8.8.84)

Ranken, John, ex Ayr, d. 1699 in Darien, reg. 1708.
(CC8.8.84)

Rate, George, in Portland, Oregon, reg. 1895. (SC70.1.337)

Reeve, Jane Bowhill, in Michaux, Powhatan Co, Virginia,
reg. 1900. (SC70.1.393)

Reid, David Boswell, physician in America, d. 5 Apr. 1863,
reg. 1865. (SC70.1.124)(H1842)

Reid, Ebenezer, teacher in Kingston, Jamaica, d. 25 May
1843, reg. 1846. (SC70.1.67)(E897)

Reid, Francis Chalmers, in Fergus, Canada, reg. 1877.
    (SC70.1.183)

Reid, James, s of William Reid & Elisabeth Meldrum in
    Parbroath, d. 25 Sep. 1843 in America, reg. 1859.
    (SC70.1.100)(H579)

Reid, Jane, at Anotto River Plantation, Jamaica, d. 29 May
    1829, reg. 1854.   (SC70.1.85)(F1958)

Reid, Margaret, in Montreal, reg. 1884.   (SC70.1.155)

Reid, Mary, in Canada, reg. 1871.   (SC70.1.155)

Reid, Robert, merchant in Falmouth, Jamaica, d. 28 Feb.
    1835, reg. 1844.   (SC70.1.66)(E890)(F134)

Reid, Robert, merchant in Jamaica, reg. 1846.   (SC70.1.67)

Reid, Robert, in New London, Connecticut, reg. 1876.
    (SC70.1.181)

Reid, Thomas, ex Edinburgh, gunner, d. 1698 in Darien,
    reg. 1708.   (CC8.8.84)

Rennie, William, in North America, reg. 1866.   (SC70.1.129)

Rhind, John, cooper in Jamaica, reg. 5 May 1789.
    (CC8.8.128)

Richardson, Ann, in Chicago, d. 1796, reg. 28 Jan. 1817.
    (CC8.8.143)

Richmond, Thomas, in Ontario, reg. 1877.   (SC70.1.184)

Rickard, William, in Kingston, St Vincent, d. 8 June 1835,
    reg. 1836.   (SC70.1.53)(D871)

Riddell, James, ex St Ninian's, sailor, d. 1698 in Darien,
    reg. 1707.   (CC8.8.83)

Riddell, Thomas, ex Leith, mariner, d. 1699 in Darien,
    reg. 1707.   (CC8.8.83)

Ritchie, George, in Barbados, d. 1790, reg. 9 Mar. 1791.
(CC8.8.128)

Ritchie, James, commission agent in New York, reg. 1873.
(SC70.1.162)

Ritchie, James Mein, in British Columbia, reg. 1879.
(SC70.1.193)

Ritchie, John, in Flatland, Restigouche, Canada, reg. 1881.
(SC70.1.205)

Ritchie, Mary, w of Rev Henry Cockburn, in Grenada, reg.
1883.   (SC70.1.228)

Ritchie, Samuel F, in Brooklyn, New York, reg. 1866.
(SC70.1.132)

Rivers, Edward, in Trinidad, d. 1810, reg. 12 June 1817.
(CC8.8.143)(SC70.1.16)

Robb, Henry, in Kingston, Jamaica, reg. 1873. (SC70.1.162)

Robb, William, in Inglis, Washington, reg. 1895.
(SC70.1.340)

Roberton, Robert, in St Thomas in the East, Surrey,
Jamaica, d. 1812, reg. 14 May 1817.   (CC8.8.143)

Robertson, Alexander, planter in Tobago, d. 16 Nov. 1814,
reg. 7 Jan. 1817.   (CC8.8.143)(SC70.1.15)

Robertson, Annie Theresa, in Amherstburg, Canada, reg. 1896.
(SC70.1.351)

Robertson, Archibald, in St Andrew, Surrey, Jamaica, d. Aug.
1800, reg. 1801.   (CC8.8.132)

Robertson, Archibald, physician & surgeon in Bellemont,
St Elizabeth, Jamaica, d. 11 Sep. 1820, reg. 1861.
(SC70.1.110(G2359)

Robertson, David, saddler in Jamaica, d. 1800, reg. 1834.
(SC70.1.50)(D601)

Robertson, David, seaman, d. 7 May 1856 in OLd Calabar River,
Jamaica, reg. 1857.   (SC70.1.93)(H248)

Robertson, Francis Lockhart, in Ontario, reg. 1896.
(SC70.1.348)

Robertson, James, physician in Barbados, reg. 1813.
(SC70.1.9)

Robertson, James, civil engineer in Jamaica, d. 14 Jan.
1829, reg. 2 July 1829. (CC8.8.152)(D54)

Robertson, John, ex Burntisland, seaman, d. 1698 in Darien,
reg. 1707. (CC8.8.83)

Robertson, John, in Bellemont, Jamaica, reg. 1823.
(SC70.1.26)

Robertson, John, ex Portobello, in Jamaica, d. 24 Sep.
1833, reg. 1834. (SC70.1.51)(D663)

Robertson, John, clerk in Toronto, reg. 1870.
(SC70.1.150)

Robertson, Patrick, s of James S Robertson, d. Sep. 1858
in Oregon, reg. 1861. (SC70.1.108)(G2205)

Robertson, Robert, in St Thomas in the East, Jamaica,
reg. 1817. (SC70.1.15)

Robertson, Robert Shiells, in Portage la Prairie, Manitoba,
reg. 1884. (SC70.1.234)

Robertson, Thomas, sailor, d. 1698 in Darien, reg. 1707.
(CC8.8.83)

Robertson, Thomas, in Ops Township, Canada, reg. 1879.
(SC70.1.194)

Robertson, William, clergyman in Blandford, Ontario,
reg. 1891. (SC70.1.300)

Robertson, William, in Carlisle Street, Newhaven,
Connecticut, reg. 1898. (SC70.1.368)

Robinson, John, merchant in Hamilton, Canada, d. 1 July
1855, reg. 1855. (SC70.1.89)(F2152)

Robinson, Neill C, merchant in the West Indies, reg. 1863.
(SC70.1.115)

Robison, Andrew, ex Berwickshire, in Montreal, d. 1 July
1842, reg. 1844. (SC70.1.64)(F10)

Rodrie, Thomas, gunner, d. 1699 in Darien, reg. 1707.
(CC8.8.83)

Rogerson, John, merchant in Quebec, d. 24 Apr. 1861, reg. 1865.
(SC70.1.127)(G4156)

Rome, Andrew, planter in St Vincent, reg. 15 Mar. 1822.
(CC8.8.148)(SC70.1.26)

Ronald, George, ex Glasgow, merchant at Cape Fear, d. 1741.
(CC8.8.107)

Ronald, William, ex Grangepans, mariner, d. 1699 in Darien,
reg. 1707. (CC8.8.83)

Ronalds, Edmund Hugh, in Florida, reg. 1895. (SC70.1.341)

Ronaldson, Janet, ex Gorgie, in Philadelphia, d. 16 Oct. 1834,
reg. 1835. (SC70.1.53)(C1384)

Rose, Isabella, in Portage la Prairie, Canada, reg. 1895.
(SC70.1.337)

Rose, John, ex Aberdeenshire, in Jamaica, d. 1 Aug. 1775,
reg. 27 Mar. 1776. (CC8.8.123)

Rose, John Pringle, in Uvas Valley, Gilroy, California,
reg. 1889. (SC70.1.272)

Ross, Alexander, ex Dumfries, draper in New York, reg. 1888.
(SC70.1.264)

Ross, Barbara, in Washington, USA, d. 10 May 1864, reg. 1865.
(SC70.1.127)(H1885)

Ross, Colin, merchant in Jamaica, d. 1779, reg. 4 May 1802.
(CC8.8.133)

Ross, David, in Baltimore, d. Sep. 1794, reg. 9 July 1804.
   (CC8.8.135)

Ross, George, in Moose Factory, North America, d. 14 May
   1846, reg. 1853.   (SC70.1.78)(F1593)

Ross, George, in Current, Eleuthera, Nassau, Bahamas,
   d. 30 May 1863, reg. 1864.   (SC70.1.122)(G3345)

Ross of Culgruff, George Clark, d. 1 Nov. 1852 in Canada,
   reg. 1857.   (SC70.1.95)(H346)

Ross, Hugh, secretary, d. pre 1708 in New England, reg.
   1708.   (CC8.8.84)

Ross, James, ex Glasgow, in Chicago, reg. 1900.
   (SC70.1.386)

Ross, James Gibb, in Bonlieve, Quebec, reg. 1890.
   (SC70.1.285)

Ross, Jessie, in Ingraham, Clinton, New York, reg. 1899.
   (SC70.1.385)

Ross, John, ex Glasgow, town officer in Montreal, reg.
   183-.   (SC70.1.48)

Ross, John, physician in Montego Bay, Jamaica, d. Sep. 1863,
   reg. 1864.   (SC70.1.120)(G3404)

Ross, Margaret, in Roscot, Fox River, Illinois, d. 22 Dec.
   1836, reg. 1838.   (SC70.1.56)(C1874)

Ross, William, ex Orkney, tailor at Hudson Bay, d. 1782,
   reg. 26 July 1784.   (CC8.8.126)

Ross, William, in St Mary's, Jamaica, d. 1802, reg. 30 Apr.
   1823.   (CC8.8.149)

Ross, William, stonecutter in Quincy, USA, reg. 1893.
   (SC70.1.322)

Roxburgh, Alexander, in Hamilton, Upper Canada, d. 5 Dec.
   1847, reg. 1848.   (SC70.1.69)(F784)

Roy, James, in Windsor, Ontario, reg. 1874. (SC70.1.167)

Ruddoch, Thomas, merchant in Tobago, d. 1790, reg. 9 Oct.
    1807.   (CC8.8.137)

Russell, Adam, in America, reg. 1878.   (SC70.1.190)

Russell, Alexander, in Manitoba, reg. 1897.   (SC70.1.360)

Russell, George, sailor, d. 1698 in Darien, reg. 1707.
    (CC8.8.83)

Russell, James, ex Edinburgh, sailor, d. 1699 in Darien,
    reg. 1707.   (CC8.8.83)

Russell, James,in San Francisco, reg. 1898.   (SC70.1.366)

Russell, John, in Boston, New England, reg. 29 Sep. 1771.
    (CC8.8.122)

Russell, Mary, in St Lucia, d. 10 Feb. 1818, reg. 6 Jan.
    1819.   (CC8.8.145)

Russell, Matthew, in Mexico, Audrian Co, Missouri, reg.
    1897.   (SC70.1.364)

Russell, William, miner in Kansas, reg. 1881. (SC70.1.211)

Rutherford, Alexander, in New York, d. 9 Nov. 1834, reg.
    1841.   (SC70.1.60)(D1444)

Rutherford, Ebenezer, carpenter in Jamaica, d. June 1804,
    reg. 15 May 1806.   (CC8.8.136)

Rutherford, George, ex Jedburgh, surgeon, d. 1698 in Darien,
    reg. 1709.   (CC8.8.84)

Rutherford, John, ex Edgeston, in USA, d. 5 Mar. 1840,
    reg. 1843.   (SC70.1.63)(C3007)

Rutherford, John Murray, in Toronto, reg. 1898.
    (SC70.1.366)

Rutherford, Margaret Craig, in Brandon, Manitoba, reg. 1900.
(SC70.1.394)

Rutherford, Thomas Scott, in St Louis, Missouri, reg. 1900.
(SC70.1.387)

Rutherford, William, in North West Territories, reg. 1897.
(SC70.1.360)

Ruthven, James Virgo, planter in Jamaica, d. 12 Oct. 1830,
reg. 1856.   (SC70.1.92)

Rymer, Janet, in Barbados, d. Nov. 1843 in Edinburgh.
(F44)

Salmond, David, in Toronto, reg. 1879.   (SC70.1.196)

Samuells, Paul Stevens, physician in Jamaica, d. 18 Nov.
    1850 in Edinburgh, reg. 1851.   (SC70.1.72)(E2498)

Sanderson, William, ex Kinghorn, soldier, d. 1699 in
    Darien, reg. 1707.   (CC8.8.83)

Sands, William, ex Dunfermline, sailor, d. 1699 in Darien,
    reg. 1707.   (CC8.8.83)

Saunders, Francis Williams, in St Louis, Potosi, Mexico,
    reg. 1886.   (SC70.1.252)

Sawers, George, farmer in Missouri, reg. 1866.   (SC70.1.130)

Sawers, John, ex Edinburgh, in Richmond, Virginia,
    d.30 Sep. 1832.   (D1299)

Schoalla, Robert, ex Orkney, carpenter, d. 1698 in Darien,
    reg. 1707.   (CC8.8.83)

Scott, Adam, in Waverly, Tioga Co, New York, reg. 1898.
    (SC70.1.382)

Scott, Alexander, clergyman in Overwharton, Stafford Co,
    Virginia, d. 1 Apr. 1738, reg. 9 Jan. 1739.
    (CC8.8.123)

Scott, Alexander, planter in Grenada, d. Feb. 1773, reg.
    12 Oct. 1775.   (CC8.8.123)

Scott, Alexander, in Tobago, d. 2 Aug. 1817, reg. 1829.
    (SC70.1.40)(D25)

Scott, Alexander, surgeon in Grenada, d. 29 Oct. 1841,
    reg. 1849.   (SC70.1.69)(F945)

Scott, Archibald, merchant in Jamaica, d. 21 Jan. 1855,
    reg. 1855.   (SC70.1.88)(F2137)

Scott, Henry, estate manager in St Vincent, d. 20 July
    1852, reg. 1854.   (SC70.1.84)(F1878)

Scott, Hugh, ex Galashiels, soldier, d. 1699 in Darien,
    reg. 1708.   (CC8.8.84)

Scott, James, ex Falkirk, mariner, d. 1698 in Darien,
    reg. 1707.   (CC8.8.83)

Scott, James, clergyman in Albany, USA, d. 22 Oct. 1852,
    reg. 1855.   (SC70.1.87)(F2071)

Scott, James, in Toronto, reg. 1897.   (SC70.1.356)

Scott, John, ex Berwickshire, d. 1699 in Darien, reg.1707.
    (CC8.8.83)

Scott, John, merchant in St John, Newfoundland, reg. 1829.
    (SC70.1.40)

Scott, Mary Brownlie, in Paterson, New Jersey, reg. 1891.
    (SC70.1.291)

Scott, Robert, ex Linlithgow, mariner, d. 1699 in Darien,
    reg. 1707.   (CC8.8.83)

Scott, Robert, in Haiti, reg. 1876.   (SC70.1.180)

Scott, Robert, in New York, reg. 1897.   (SC70.1.364)

Scott, Thomas, Chief Justice of Upper Canada, reg. 1873.
    (SC70.1.163)

Scott, Thomas, in Owen Sound, Canada, reg. 1884.   (SC70.1.237)

Scott, Walter, book-keeper in the West Indies, d. Sep. 1802,
    reg. 30 July 1807.   (CC8.8.137)

Scott, William, master of the "Charlotte of Boston", reg.
    27 Mar. 1780.   (CC8.8.125)

Scott, William, advocate in Quebec, d. 5 Jan. 1820, reg. 1820.
    (CC8.8.146)

Scott, William, in Savannah, Georgia, d. 14 July 1830 in
    Liverpool, reg. 1831.   (SC70.1.45)(C499)

Scott, William, in Grenada, d. 1 Dec. 1846, reg. 1849.
    (SC70.1.69)(F908)

Scouller, Christian, w of Rev Matthew Wilson, in Sidney
    Mills, Cape Breton, Nova Scotia, d. 28 Mar. 1852,
    reg. 1853.   (SC70.1.79)(E3373)

Scrogie, Alexander, sailor, d. 1699 in Darien, reg. 1707.
    (CC8.8.83)

Scrogie, Robert, sailor, d. 1698 in Darein, reg. 1707.
    (CC8.8.83)

Seaton, John, ex Berwickshire, clergyman, d. 1698 in Darien,
    reg. 1707.   (CC8.8.83)

Selby, Thomas, ex Edinburgh, d. Jamaica, reg. 1829.
    (SC70.1.41)

Seller, Patrick, ex Selkirk, manufacturer in Colorado,
    reg. 1891.   (SC70.1.301)

Seranda, Joanes, sailor, d. 1698 in Darien, reg. 1707.
    (CC8.8.83)

Seton, Alexander, clerk, d. 1698 in Darien, reg. 1708.
    (CC8.8.84)

Seton, George, ex Burntisland, sailor, d. 1698 in Darien,
    reg. 1707.   (CC8.8.83)

Seton, John, in Jamaica, reg. 7 Nov. 1797.   (CC8.8.130)

Shairp, Robert, soldier, d. 1699 in Darien, reg. 1707.
    (CC8.8.83)

Shairp, Thomas, in the West Indies, d. 1805, reg. 25 Oct.
    1812.   (CC8.8.138)

Shand, John Harvey, in Grenada, d. 25 Nov. 1857, reg. 1860.
    (SC70.1.105)(G1821)

Shaw, Alexander, manager in Nutmeg Grove, Tobago,
    d. 1 Dec. 1832, reg. 1834.   (SC70.1.51)(D695)

Shaw, Alexander, in Jamaica, reg. 1869.   (SC70.1.145)

Shaw, James Allan, clergyman in Arichat, Richmond Co,
    Nova Scotia, d. 22 Apr. 1860, reg. 1861.
    (SC70.1.110)(G2430)

Shaw, John, carpenter in Grenada, d. 21 Aug. 1794, reg.
    25 Aug. 1795.   (CC8.8.130)

Shaw, Lachlan, soldier in South Carolina, d. 1761, reg.
    1 Dec. 1762.   (CC8.8.119)

Shaw, William, in Chrystal City, Missouri, d. Edinburgh,
    reg. 1892.   (SC70.1.305)

Shawe, Robert, in Kingston, Jamaica, d. 15 Oct. 1818 in
    London.   (C430)

Shirreff, Robert, in New York, d. 18 Aug. 1847 in St Croix,
    reg. 1859.   (SC70.1.101)(G1452)

Shivaz, George, in Antigua, d. Apr. 1795 in Borthwick,
    reg. 22 Apr. 1796.   (CC9.7.76)

Shives, Thomas, clerk in Brooklyn, reg. 1890.   (SC70.1.283)

Short, James, in Virginia, reg. 26 Sep. 1787.   (CC8.8.127)

Shortreid, John, in Virginia, d. 1792, reg. 29 Jan. 1801.
    (CC8.8.132)

Sibley, George, in New Jersey, reg. 1876.   (SC70.1.177)

Sime, Archibald, ex Bo'ness, sailor, d. 1699 in Darien,
    reg. 1707.   (CC8.8.83)

Simms, Jacob, in Trinidad, reg. 1823.   (SC70.1.29)

Simpson, Alexande, ex Dysart, mariner, d. 1698 in Darien,
    reg. 1707.   (CC8.8.83)

Simpson, David, merchant in Jamaica, d.in London, reg. 19 July 1756. (CC8.8.116)

Simpson, George, clerk in Grenada, d. 1775, reg. 8 Feb. 1779. (CC8.8.124)

Simpson, Jane, w of George Russell, in USA, reg. 1836. (SC70.1.54)

Simpson, John, in New York, d. Nov. 1784, reg. 26 May 1785. (CC8.8.126)

Simpson, Joseph, in Toronto, reg. 1899. (SC70.1.379)

Simpson, Patrick, planter in John's Island, South Carolina, d. 1791, reg. 5 Feb. 1794. (CC8.8.129)(B59.38.6.195)

Simpson, William, ex Edinburgh, sailor,d. 1699 in Darien, reg. 1707. (CC8.8.83)

Sims, William, in New Town of San Juan, Cuba, d. 21 Mar. 1860, reg. 1862. (SC70.1.113)(G2757)

Simson, Thomas, ex Fife, d. 1699 in Darien, reg. 1708. (CC8.8.84)

Sinclair, David, mariner in Jamaica, reg. 10 July 1733. (CC8.8.95)

Sinclair, John, ex Inverkip, mariner, d. 1699 in Darien, reg. 1707. (CC8.8.83)

Sivewright, David, in St Thomas, Jamaica, d. 15 Nov. 1847, reg. 1852. (SC70.1.74)(E2924)

Sivewright, Henrietta Home, in Lower Norton, King's Co, New Brunswick, reg. 1884. (SC70.1.236)

Sivewright, John, of the Hudson Bay Company, d. 4 Sep. 1856 in Edinburgh. (G354)

Skene, Robert, in Maryland, d. 1736, reg. 20 Oct. 1741. (CC8.8.105)

Sleiman, Gabriel, ex Paisley, sailor, d. 1699 in Darien,
    reg. 1707.   (CC8.8.83)

Sloan, Elizabeth, in Salt Lake City, reg. 1888.   (SC70.1.265)

Smellie, George William, in Florida, reg. 1875.   (SC70.1.175)

Smith, Andrew, in Jamaica, d. in Edinburgh, reg. 17 Dec.1788.
    (CC8.8.127)

Smith, Andrew, merchant in Barbados, reg. 1822.   (SC70.1.26)

Smith, Arthur Everard, in Omaha, Nebraska, reg. 1893.
    (SC70.1.323)

Smith, George, sailor in New York, reg. 1857.   (SC70.1.94)

Smith, George, ex Dumfries, clerk in Coney Island, New York,
    reg. 1888.   (SC70.1.269)

Smith, George, in Cherrybank Farm, Saltfleet, Ontario,
    reg. 1891.   (SC70.1.299)

Smith, John, ex Haddington, sailor, d. 1699 in Darien,
    reg. 1707.   (CC8.8.83)

Smith, James, overseer in Tobago, d. 3 Apr. 1853, reg. 1854.
    (SC70.1.85)

Smith, James, in Nichol, Wellington, Ontario, reg. 1895.
    (SC70.1.344)

Smith, James, in New Millport, Ohio, reg. 1896.
    (SC70.1.346)

Smith, John, Captain in US Navy, d. 1 Sep. 1815, reg.
    7 Mar. 1825.   (CC8.8.150)(SC70.1.32)

Smith, John, planter in Jamaica, reg. 1872.   (SC70.1.158)

Smith, John, in 3rd Avenue, New York, reg. 1898.
    (SC70.1.368)

Smith, John Malcolm, clergyman in Kingston, Canada, d. 8 Aug.
    1856, reg. 1857.   (SC70.1.93)(G442)

Smith, John Murray, in Geneva, USA, reg. 1870. (SC70.1.148)

Smith, Livingston, in South Carolina, d. 1831, reg. 1841.
(SC70.1.61)(D1497)

Smith, Margaret, in North Parma, New York, reg. 1876.
(SC70.1.181)

Smith, Mary Dryden, in London, Canada, reg. 1871.
(SC70.1.154)

Smith, Matthew, ex Irvine, ships carpenter in Pasquatank,
Carolina, reg. 30 May 1771. (CC8.8.122)

Smith, Samuel, in Halifax, Nova Scotia, d. 27 Mar. 1844,
reg. 1845. (SC70.1.66)(F222)

Smith, Thomas Adam, in Williamsport, Pennsylvania, reg.
1887. (SC70.1.258)

Smith, William, ex Monifieth, schoolmaster in Canada,
reg. 1892. (SC70.1.302)

Smith, William Gall, in Galt, Ontario, reg. 1897.
(SC70.1.357)

Smyth, William James, in Kankakee, Illinois, reg. 1870.
(SC70.1.147)

Snell, William, in San Antonio, Texas, reg. 1876.
(SC70.1.177)

Snodgrass, Neil, ex Paisley, merchant in Virginia, d. 1782,
reg. 10 Apr. 1788. (CC8.8.127)

Somerville, David, ex Strathaven, clergyman in North
America, reg. 22 Feb. 1799. (CC8.8.131)

Somerville, William, ex Culross, sailor, d. 1698 in Darien,
reg. 1707. (CC8.8.83)

Spalsie, John, ex Kirkcudbright, surgeon, d. 1699 in
Darien, reg. 1708. (CC8.8.84)

Spence, John, ex Leith, sailor, d. 1699 in Darien, reg. 1707.
(CC8.8.83)

Spence, John, in Quebec, d. 24 Oct. 1829.   (C236)

Spence, John, carpenter in Vancouver Island, reg. 1866.
(SC70.1.130)

Spence, Margaret, in Avon Cottage, Peterborough, Ontario,
reg. 1884.   (SC70.1.233)

Spence, William, in Ontario, reg. 1896.   (SC70.1.350)

Spencer, Ambrose Hall, in Los Angeles, reg. 1896.
(SC70.1.350)

Spittal, William, in St Thomas, Jamaica, d. 21 Nov. 1837,
reg. 1841.   (SC70.1.60)(C2562)

Spreull, Samuel, merchant in Toronto, reg. 1881.
(SC70.1.206)

Sproule, Andrew, merchant in Gosport, Norfolk, Virginia,
reg. 22 Jan. 1779.   (CC8.8.124)

Stark, Adam Bertram, in David Co, USA, reg. 1893.
(SC70.1.316)

Staunton, Moses, in Toronto, reg. 1878.   (SC70.1.188)

Steel, Hugh, ex Bo'ness, shipmaster in Philadelphia,
d. 1757, reg. 13 Feb. 1759.   (CC8.8.118)

Steel, John, sailor, d. 1699 in Darien, reg. 1708.
(CC8.8.83)

Steele, Alexander, in Southwold, Canada, reg. 1892.
(SC70.1.309)

Stenhouse, George, ex Burntisland, sailor, d. 1698 in
Darien, reg. 1707.   (CC8.8.83)

Stephen, Alexander Reid, farmer in Texas, reg. 1879.
(SC70.1.193)

Stephen, James, surgeon in Hamilton, Canada, d. 6 Nov. 1857,
(G908)

Stephen, William, farmer in Texas, reg. 1879. (SC70.1.197)

Stephenson, William, ex Newmills, in St James, Jamaica,
d. 18 June 1835. (F692)

Steven, William, ex Aberdeenshire, in Jamaica, reg. 24 Jan.
1740. (CC8.8.103)

Stevenson, Agnes, ex Edinburgh, in San Francisco, reg. 1887.
(SC70.1.258)

Stevenson, Andrew McMath, in San Francisco, reg. 1891.
(SC70.1.299)

Stevenson, Archibald, ex Wigtownshire, farmer in America,
reg. 1887. (SC70.1.256)

Stevenson, Hamilton, painter in Charleston, South Carolina,
d. 1783 in Jamaica, reg. 29 Mar. 1788. (CC8.8.127)

Stevenson, Henry, in Jamaica, d. 7 July 1845. (F699)

Stevenson, James, sailor, d. 1698 in Darien, reg. 1707.
(CC8.8.83)

Stevenson, James, planter in Jamaica, d. 24 May 1844, reg.
1847. (SC70.1.67)(E1165)

Stevenson, James, in Tobago, d. 17 Sep. 1848, reg. 1856.
(SC70.1.92)(G286)

Stevenson, Jean, in Charleston, South Carolina, d. 1783
in Jamaica, reg. 8 July 1796. (CC8.8.130)

Stevenson, John, ex Culross, quartermaster,d. 1699 in
Darien, reg. 1708. (CC8.8.84)

Stevenson, Polly, in Scarborough, Tobago, d. 27 Dec. 1855,
    reg. 1856. (SC70.1.91)(G254)

Stevenson, Robert Louis, in Samoa, reg. 1897. (SC70.1.277)

Stevenson, William, in New York, reg. 1889. (SC70.1.277)

Stewart, Adolphus, merchant in Brooklyn, New York, d. 1822,
    reg. 21 Apr. 1824. (CC8.8.150)(SC70.1.27)

Stewart, Alexander, ex Kincarrochie, tailor, d. 1698 in
    Darien, reg. 1707. (CC8.8.83)

Stewart, Alexander, surgeon in Chambersburg, Franklin Co,
    Pennsylvania, reg. 24 Jan. 1794. (CC8.8.129)

Stewart, Andrew Burns, in Aux Cayes, Haiti, reg. 1867.
    (SC70.1.136)

Stewart, Archibald, planter in Dominica, d. 1777, reg.
    11 Oct. 1798. (CC8.8.131)

Stewart, Daniel, ex West Lothian, sailor, d. 1698 in Darien,
    reg. 1707. (CC8.8.83)

Stewart, Elizabeth, in Philadelphia, reg. 1897. (SC70.1.356)

Stewart, Francis, in St David's, Jamaica, d. 10 July 1864,
    reg. 1865. (SC70.1.125)(H1860)

Stewart, George, ex South Uist, book-keeper in New York,
    reg. 1892. (SC70.1.313)

Stewart, James, judge in Halifax, Nova Scotia, d. 5 Feb. 1830,
    reg. 1839. (SC70.1.43)

Stewart, James Campbell, in Canada, reg. 1878. (SC70.1.190)

Stewart, John, soldier, d. 1699 in Darien, reg. 1707.
    (CC8.8.83)

Stewart, John Andrew, master mariner in New Jersey, reg. 1896.
    (SC70.1.343)

Stewart, Malcolm, in Jamaica, d. 13 Nov. 1840 in Edinburgh.
   (C2489)

Stewart, Margaret, in Brooklyn, reg. 1893.   (SC70.1.316)

Stewart, Neil, in Halifax, Nova Scotia, reg. 1 Mar. 1793.
   (CC8.8.129)

Stewart, Robert, merchant in Petersburg, Virginia, reg.
   13 Apr. 1816.   (CC8.8.142)

Stewart, William, in Cuba, reg. 6 Sep. 1791.   (CC8.8.128)

Stirling, Alexander, ex Port of Menteith, d. 1699 in
   Darien, reg. 1710.   (CC8.8.84)

Stirling, James, merchant in Montreal, d. 1 June 1861, reg.
   1862.   (SC70.1.112)(G2625)

Stirling, Robert, ex Glasgow, merchant, d. Darien, reg.
   1707.   (CC8.8.83)

Stoddart, David, in Tobago, d. 2 Apr. 1831 in Portobello.
   (C457)

Storie, Francis, ex Linlithgow, soldier, d. 1699 in the
   West Indies, reg. 1707.   (CC8.8.83)

Stormonth, James, in St Kitts, reg. 24 Dec. 1761.
   (CC8.8.118)

Strachan, Alexander, in St Louis, USA, reg. 1873.   (SC70.1.160)

Strachan, Alexander, banker in Montreal, reg. 1883.
   (SC70.1.224)

Strachan, William, in Halifax, Nova Scotia, reg. 1842.
   (SC70.1.62)

Strange, Eliza, in Canada West, reg. 1866.   (SC70.1.128)

Strange, James Maxwell, in Toronto, reg. 1867.   (SC70.1.134)

Strange, John, in Kingston, Upper Canada, reg. 1866.
(SC70.1.128)

Strange, John Maxwell, in Canada, reg. 1870.   (SC70.1.148)

Strong, Janet, in Iowa, reg. 1897.   (SC70.1.356)

Sprott, Margaret, in Hamfield, Westmoreland Co, Pennsylvania, reg. 1900.   (SC70.1.393)

Stephens, John George, in Prospect, Los Angeles, California,
reg. 1898.   (SC70.1.371)

Strangeways, Christopher, ex Leith, in Downingtown,
Pennsylvania, reg. 1899.   (SC70.1.377)

Stuart, Christopher,ex Leith, merchant in Carolina, reg.
1718.   (CC8.8.87)

Stuart, Charles, ex Leith, merchant in Carolina, reg. 1718.
(CC8.8.87)

Stuart, Charles, merchant in Birkhall, Canada West, reg.
1874.   (SC70.1.168)

Stuart, David Knox, physician in New Orleans, d. May 1851,
reg. 1853.   (SC70.1.81)

Stuart, John, ex Leith, merchant in Carolina, reg. 1718.
(CC8.8.87)

Stuart, William, plumber in Montreal, reg. 1871.
(SC70.1.151)

Sushan, William, ex Edinburgh, yeoman, d. 1698 in Darien,
reg. 1707.   (CC8.8.83)

Sutherland, Donald, in Jamaica, reg. 27 Nov. 1801.
(CC8.8.132)

Sutherland, John, ex Falkirk, boot & shoe maker in New York,
reg. 1888.   (SC70.1.271)

Sutherland, William Smith, in California, reg. 1867.
      (SC70.1.137)

Suttie, David, ex Kirkcaldy, mariner, d. 1698 in Darien,
      reg. 1707.   (CC8.8.83)

Swanston, Thomas, physician in St Kitts, reg. 1874.
      (SC70.1.166)

Swinton, Alexander, ex Glasgow, soldier, d. 6 Feb. 1699 in
      Darien, reg. 1707.   (CC8.8.83)

Syme, John, ex Earlsferry, cook, d. 1699 in Darien, reg.
      1707.   (CC8.8.83)

Symington, Mary, in Rocky Point, Suffolk Co, New York,
      reg. 1887.   (SC70.1.259)

Tait, James, ex Burntisland, seaman, d. 1698 in Darien, reg. 1707. (CC8.8.83)

Tait, Peter, in Tobago, d. 9 July 1859, reg. 1860. (SC70.1.103)(G1616)

Tait, Robert, physician in Antigua, d. 16 Aug. 1845, reg. 1846. (SC70.1.66)(E618)

Tasker, Patrick, merchant in St John's, Newfoundland, d. 2 Nov. 1860, reg. 1861. (SC70.1.108)(G2195)

Taylor, Alexander, ex Burntisland, seaman, d. 1698 in Darien, reg. 1707. (CC8.8.83)

Taylor, Alexander, in Broadway, New York, reg. 1899. (SC70.1.379)

Taylor, Archibald, ex Doune, in Tobago, reg. 28 Feb. 1775. (CC8.8.123)

Taylor, George Henry, in St Vincent, reg. 1873. (SC70.1.165)

Taylor, Isabella, in Brooklyn, reg. 1900. (SC70.1.387)

Taylor, John, goldsmith in St Eustatia, reg. 18 Nov. 1784. (CC8.8.126)

Taylor, John, cabinet-maker in New Providence, d. 13 Sep. 1794, reg. 29 Apr. 1796. (CC8.8.130)

Taylor, John, in Bardowie, Jamaica, d. 1800, reg. 1831. (SC70.1.45)(D279)

Taylor, John, in Ontario, reg. 1882. (SC70.1.216)

Taylor, John Rae, in 21 Vine Street, Brooklyn, New York, reg. 1885. (SC70.1.240)

Taylor, John Swanston, in Quebec, reg. 1873. (SC70.1.161)

Taylor, Peter Burnet, in New York, reg. 1899. (SC70.1.378)

Templeton, James, in Dane, USA, reg. 1878. (SC70.1.193)

Templeton, Thomas, in Chicago, reg. 1882. (SC70.1.214)

Thirde, James Young, clergyman in Huntsville, Ontario,
    reg. 1884. (SC70.1.234)

Thom, William, ex Bute, in Dundas, Canada West, d. 4 May
    1860. (G2221)

Thomas, Charles, in Washington, reg. 1893. (SC70.1.329)

Thompson, William Dick, in Perth, Ontario, reg. 1895.
    (SC70.1.337)

Thomson, Agnes, in Jamaica, d. 19 Dec. 1850, reg. 1852.
    (SC70.1.77)(F1553)

Thomson, Andrew, ex Leith, sailor, d. 1698 in Darien,
    reg. 1707. (CC8.8.83)

Thomson, Andrew, clergyman in Virginia, reg. 3 May 1727.
    (CC8.8.91)

Thomson, David, baillie of Inverkeithing, d. 1698 in
    Darien, reg. 1707. (CC8.8.83)

Thomson, Dugald, ex Cardross, in Jamaica, reg. 6 Dec. 1823.
    (CC9.7.81)

Thomson, Emily Ida, in Michigan, reg. 1882. (SC70.1.218)

Thomson, Henry, sailor, d. 1698 in Darien, reg. 1707.
    (CC8.8.83)

Thomson, Henry Lawson, in Brooklyn, New York, reg. 1880.
    (SC70.1.203)

Thomson, James, ex Aberdour, sailor, d. 1699 in Darien,
    reg. 1707. (CC8.8.83)

Thomson, James, ex Edinburgh, sailor, d. 1698 in Darien,
    reg. 1707. (CC8.8.83)

Thomson, James, in Cornwall, Jamaica, d. 1 Jan. 1829, reg. 1831.   (SC70.1.43)(C334)

Thomson, James, in Emporia, Kansas, reg. 1884. (SC70.1.231)

Thomson, James, in Quebec, reg. 1889.   (SC70.1.279)

Thomson, Jean, in Rosenden, Cairo, Illinois, reg. 1853. (SC70.1.79)

Thomson, Jessie, in Chicago, reg. 1893.   (SC70.1.321)

Thomson, John, farmer in Nepean, Canada,d. 24 Dec. 1830. (E655)

Thomson, John, in Frankfort Station, Will Co, Illinois, reg. 1884.   (SC70.1.237)

Thomson, Maria,in Washington, DC, reg. 1889.   (SC70.1.279)

Thomson, Marion, in St Kitts, d. 20 Apr. 1818, reg. 23 June 1819.   (CC8.8.145)

Thomson, Mary, in Chicago, reg. 1896.   (SC70.1.315)

Thomson, Patrick, s of Andrew Thomson advocate in Edinburgh, writer & merchant in the Bahamas, reg. 10 June 1720. (CC8.8.87)

Thomson, Walter, ex Bo'ness, sailor, d. 1699 in Darien, reg. 1709.   (CC8.8.84)

Thomson, William, ex Hopetoun, sailor, d. 1699 in Darien, reg.1707.   (CC8.8.83)

Thomson, William, ex Irvine, sailor, d. 1699 in Darien, reg. 1710.   (CC8.8.84)

Thomson, William, merchant in Kingston, Jamaica, reg. 25 Oct. 1783.   (CC8.8.126)

Thomson, William Conn, in Kingston, New York, reg. 1867.
(SC70.1.136)

Thorburn, Andrew, in Detroit, d. 16 June 1849, reg. 1850.
(SC70.1.70)(E2254)

Thornborrow, George, in Cumberland Co, New Jersey,
reg. 1897. (SC70.1.360)

Thwaites, Jane, in Salt Lake City, reg. 1895. (SC70.1.342)

Tocher, Alexander, in Colorado, reg. 1896. (SC70.1.348)

Tod, Matthew, in St Louis, reg. 1869. (SC70.1.141)

Tod, William Robert, in Saranne Lake, Franklin Co, New York,
reg. 1889. (SC70.1.281)

Torrance, John, editor in New York, d. 2 June 1858,
reg. 1860. (SC70.1.105)(H887)

Toward, Henry, ex Bo'ness, seaman, d. 1698 in Darien,
reg. 1707. (CC8.8.83)

Towart, Robert, ex Dundee, hat manufacturer in New York,
d. 1836, reg. 1839. (SC70.1.58)(D1216)

Tower, Ann, ex Edinburgh, in St Croix, d. 8 Jan. 1843.
C2078)

Trakes, Maxwell, in Richmond, Virginia, d. 4 Dec. 1852,
reg. 1853. (SC70.1.79)(E3428)

Traquair, James, ex Torpichen, sailor, d. 1698 in Darien,
reg. 1707. (CC8.8.83)

Trotter, George, in Springfield, USA, d. 18 May 1842,
reg. 1843. (SC70.1.64)(C3218)

Troup, James, ex Edinburgh, sailor, d. 1699 in Darien,
reg. 1707. (CC8.8.83)

126

Truefitt, Henry Paul, in Philadelphia, d. 12 May 1864,
    reg. 1865. (SC70.1.127)(G4132)

Turnbull, Catherine, in San Bernardino, California, reg.
    1888. (SC70.1.267)

Turnbull, George, planter in Grenada,d. 24 Jan. 1809,
    reg. 24 Oct. 1809. (CC8.8.137)(SC70.1.1)

Turnbull, James, in Antigua, reg. 1817. (SC70.1.15)

Turnbull, Peter, planter in Montserrat, reg. 22 June 1809.
    (SC53.56.1)

Turnbull, Thomas, in Antigua, reg. 20 Mar. 1817. (CC8.8.143)

Turnbull, William, mariner, d. 1698 in Darien, reg. 1707.
    (CC8.8.83)

Turner, James, ex Alloway, sailor, d. 1699 in Darien, reg.
    1707. (CC8.8.83)

Turner, Louis Paulo, in Seymour, Canada, d. 15 Apr. 1844,
    reg. 1847. (SC70.1.68)(F566)

Turner, Robert, ex Greenock, in Montreal, d. 7 Jan. 1836,
    reg. 1837. (SC70.1.54)(C1590)

Turriff, Isabella, in the West Indies, reg. 1881.
    (SC70.1.211)

Twatt, Magnus, in York, Hudson Bay, d. 23 Oct. 1801, reg.
    24 Sep. 1804. (CC8.8.135)

Underwood, Francis Henry, US Consul, reg. 1894.
(SC70.1.335)

Urquhart, George, in Houston, Texas, reg. 1893.
(SC70.1.325)

Urquhart, John, in Hamilton, Ontario, reg. 1894.
(SC70.1.334)

Van Baerle, Thomas John, in Stamford, Upper Canada, d. 28 Dec.
1837, reg. 1823.   (SC70.1.56)(C1934)

Vass, Charles, ex Edinburgh, sailor, d. 1698 in Darien, reg.
1707.   (CC8.8.83)

Veatch, William, ex Dumfries, d. 1699 in Darien, reg. 1709.
(CC8.8.84)

Vere, John Weir, Commissary in St Vincent, reg. 24 Jan. 1781.
(CC8.8.125)

Vertue, James, supercargo, d. 1799 in New Providence.
(CC9.7.77)

Virtue, Daniel, planter in Jamaica, d. 16 Nov. 1823, reg.
1836.   (SC70.1.54)(C1552)

Waddell, Duncan, in Dartmouth, Nova Scotia, reg. 1893.
   (SC70.1.321)

Waddell, George, ex Burntisland, in Denver, Colorado, reg.
   1899. (SC70.1.377)

Waddell, Thomas, ex Prestonpans, sailor, d. 1699 in Darien,
   reg. 1707. (CC8.8.83)

Wale, James, mate of St Peter of New York, d. Apr. 1692 in
   England, reg. 18 Jun. 1692. (CC8.8.79)

Walker, Adam, ex Edinburgh, tailor, d. 1698 in Darien, reg.
   1707. (CC8.8.82)

Walker, Christina, in Camp Hall, Virginia, d. 30 Mar. 1861,
   reg. 1864. (SC70.1.121)(H1693)

Walker, George, ex Edinburgh, butcher, d. 1698 in Darien, reg.
   1707. (CC8.8.83)

Walker, George, in New Orleans, d. 18 Aug. 1851, reg. 1857.
   (SC70.1.95)(H327)

Walker, James, in St Ann, Jamaica, d. 31 Oct. 1827. (C160)

Walker, James, ex Montrose, in Jamaica, reg. 1826.
   (SC70.1.34)

Walker, James, customs collector in Nassau, d. 15 Apr. 1838
   in Edinburgh, reg. 1840. (SC70.1.53)(C2287)

Walker, James Dennistoun, in Antigua, reg. 1886. (SC70.1.248)

Walker, John, merchant in New Providence, Bahamas, reg. 3 Dec.
   1792. (CC8.8.129)

Walker, John, merchant in St John, New Brunswick, reg. 1871.
   (SC70.1.154)

Walker, Robert, in Haiti, reg. 1876. (SC70.1.180)

Walker, Robert, in San Rafael, Marin County, California, reg.
   1898. (SC70.1.367)

Walker, William, ex Fife, sailor, d. 1698 in Darien, reg. 1707. (CC8.8.83)

Wallace, John, ex Edinburgh, engineer, d. 1699 in Darien, reg. 1707. (CC8.8.83)

Wallace, John, ex Musselburgh, quartermaster, d. 1698 in Darien, reg. 1707. (CC8.8.83)

Wallace, John, in Blenheim, Canada West, d. 9 Sep. 1854, reg. 1854. (SC70.1.84)(E4007)

Ward, Elizabeth Witty, in Platte, Cater, Nebraska, reg. 1893. (SC70.1.322)

Wardrop, John, merchant in Brunswick County, Virginia, reg. 25 Jul. 1791. (CC8.8.128)

Wardrop, William, s of David Wardrop and Mary Bogle, ex Glasgow, d. 1848 in West Indies. (SC70.1.17)

Warrack, James, ex Edinburgh, sailor, d. 169 in Darien, reg. 1707. (CC8.8.83)

Warrender, William, ex Wemyss, mariner, d. 1698 in Darien, reg. 1707. (CC8.8.83)

Waters, John, in St Mary, Jamaica, d. Mar. 1834, reg. 1834. (SC70.1.51)(C1125)

Waterstone, James R, in New York, reg. 1867. (SC70.1.137)

Watkins, Eliza, in Canada West, reg. 1866. (SC70.1.128)

Watson, Alexander, ex Glasgow, in America, d. Jul. 1857. (SC70.1.96)(H390)

Watson, George, in Jamaica, d. 3 Apr. 1835, reg. 1835 (SC70.1.53)(C1369)

Watson, Hugh, in Crestfluie, Cherokee County, Kansas, reg. 1898. (SC70.1.370)

Watson, Isabella, wid of John Cullen, d. 3 Apr. 1834 in Jamaica, reg. 1854. (SC70.1.82)(F1815)

Watson, Isabella, in New York, reg. 1894.   (SC70.1.329)

Watson, Jmes, ex Burntisland, sailor, d. 1698 in Darien, reg.
    1707.   (CC8.8.83)

Watson, James, in Toronto, d. 9 Apr. 1845, reg. 1848.
    (SC70.1.68)(E1377)

Watson, James, farmer in Harlaw, Nebraska, reg. 1900.
    (SC70.1.389)

Watson, Janet, in White Plains, New York, d. 12 Feb. 1859,
    reg. 1860.   (SC70.1.103)(G1619)

Watson, James McNair, commission agent in Havana, d. 16 Jan.
    1849 in Edinburgh, reg. 1849.   (SC70.1.69)(F858)

Watson, Janet, in Brantford, Canada West, d. 3 Apr. 1834, reg.
    1866.   (SC70.1.129)

Watson, John, merchant in Charleston, South Carolina, reg.
    21 Dec. 1756.   (CC8.8.116)

Watson, Marion, in Toronto, reg. 1877.   (SC70.1.183)

Watt, Ebenezer, ironfounder in New York, d. Jersey City, reg.
    1881.   (SC70.1.205)

Watt, John, ex Newcastle, armorer, d. 1698 in Darien, reg.
    1707.   (CC8.8.83)

Watt, Thomas, ex Fife, mariner, d. 1698 in Darien, reg. 1707.
    (CC8.8.83)

Weatherly, Herbert, in Washington, reg. 1892.   (SC70.1.311)

Webster, Robert, in Jamaica, reg. 1846.   (SC70.1.67)

Weddel, James, in New York, reg. 1877.   (SC70.1.185)

Wederstone, James R, in New York, reg. 1867.   (SC70.1.137)

Weir, George, in Kaines, Canada, d. 23 Nov. 1837.   (C2073)

Weir, John, ex Edinburgh, gunner, d. 1699 in Darien, reg.
     1707.   (CC8.8.83)

Weir, Thomas, merchant in Jamaica, d. London, reg. 14 Jun.
     1740.   (CC8.8.103)

Weir, William, merchant in St Vincent, d. 8 May 1795, reg.
     18 May 1798.   (CC8.8.131)

Welsh, James Henry, accountant in Montreal, reg. 1893.
     (SC70.1.320)

Welsh, John Miller, in Andover, USA, reg. 1893.   (SC70.1.316)

Wemyss, James, soldier, d. 1699 in Darien, reg. 1707.
     (CC8.8.83)

Wemyss, John, ex Edinburgh, sailor, d. 1698 in Darien, reg.
     1707.   (CC8.8.83)

Westland, David Douglas, ex Edinburgh, civil engineer in
     Salma Cruz, Mexico, reg. 1900.   (SC70.1.396)

Wetmore, Margaret, in Wood County, Ohio, reg. 1885.
     (SC70.1.240)

White, Andrew, in Pickering, Upper Canada, d. 20 Aug. 1832,
     reg. 1842.   (SC70.1.61)

White, Andrew, plumber in Old Harbor, Jamaica, reg. 1854.
     (SC70.1.82)

Whitelaw, David, seaman in Drycreek, California, d. Nov. 1850,
     reg. 1856.   (SC70.1.92)(H188)

Whitfield, George, clergyman in Georgia, reg. 3 Jun. 1774.
     (CC8.8.123)

Whitton, Alexander Barry, in Detroit, reg. 1884.   (SC70.1.237)

Whitton, James, in Brooklyn, reg. 1895.   (SC70.1.338)

Whyte, Archibald, ex Clackmannan, sailor, d. 1699 in Darien, reg. 1708. (CC8.8.84)

Whyte, John, in Hull, Ottawa, reg. 1888. (SC70.1.268)

Whyte, John, ex Perthshire, in Chicago, reg. 1891. (SC70.1.330)

Wigglesworth, John, in Ontario, reg. 1871. (SC70.1.152)

Wight, Alexander, merchant in Jamaica, reg. 19 Sep. 1785. (CC8.8.127)

Wightman, Charles, in Tobago, d. 31 Dec. 1830 in Edinburgh. (C952)

Wighton, Henry, ex Kirkcaldy, mariner, d. 1698 in Darien, reg 1707. (CC8.8.83)

Wilkes, Anne, in Hain, Ontario, reg. 1891. (SC70.1.331)

Wilkie, David, ex Glasgow, in Jamaica, d. 12 Oct. 1808, reg. 13 Apr. 1809. (CC8.8.137)

Wilkie, Thomas, ex Glasgow, merchant in Kingston, Jamaica, d. 1794 in Jamaica, reg. 22 Nov. 1794. (CC8.8.129)

Williams, Thomas, ex Leith, mariner, d. 1698 in Darien, reg. 1707. (CC8.8.83)

Williamson, Alexander, ex Northfield, Edinburgh, in New Orleans, d. 3 Oct. 1838, reg. 1852. (SC70.1.75)(F1409)

Williamson, John, ex Cardenden, sailor, d. 1698 in Darien, reg. 1707. (CC8.8.83)

Williamson, Margaret, in America, d. 31 Feb. 1824, reg. 1823. (CC8.8.150)(SC70.1.29)

Williamson, Walter, surgeon in Stafford, St Paul, Virginia, reg. 22 Jun. 1776. (CC8.8.123)

Wilson, Agnes, in Petersburg, Virginia, reg. 1876. (SC70.1.181)

Wilson, Charles, ex Fife, mariner, d. 1698 in Darien,
    reg. 1707.   (CC8.8.83)

Wilson, Charles, planter in Trelawney, Jamaica, d. 25 Mar.
    1843, reg. 1844.   (SC70.1.66)(E229)

Wilson, David, ex Wemyss, sailor, d. 1698 in Darien,
    reg. 1707.   (CC8.8.83)

Wilson, Elizabeth, in Barbados, d. 26 Oct. 1841.   (D1618)

Wilson, George, ex Dysart, sailor, d. 1699 in Darien, reg.
    1707.   (CC8.8.83)

Wilson, George, mason in Roslyn Castle, Jamaica,
    d. 9 Mar. 1834, reg. 1834.   (SC70.1.51)(D652)

Wilson, George, pilot in Charleston, South Carolina,
    reg. 1886.   (SC70.1.249)

Wilson, James, ex Leith, shipowner, d. 25 June 1840 in
    Tobago.   (D1678)

Wilson, James, in Holy Cross, Dakota Territory, reg. 1874.
    (SC70.1.1169)

Wilson, James, in Guelph, d. Wellington, Ontario, reg. 1884.
    (SC70.1.230)

Wilson, John, ex Fife, mariner, d. 1698 in Darien, reg. 1708.
    (CC8.8.84)

Wilson, Jòhn, planter in Arona, Trinidad, d. 26 Apr. 1833,
    reg. 1835.   (SC70.1.52)(C1327)

Wilson, John, Postmaster General of Jamaica, reg. 1851.
    (SC70.1.73)

Wilson, John Black, miner in Pennsylvania, reg. 1893.
    (SC70.1.321)

Wilson, John Buchanan, commission agent in 120 Water Street,
    New York, d. 30 May 1855, reg. 1855.   (SC70.1.88)(E4394)

Wilson, Margaret, in Barbados, reg. 1842.   (SC70.1.62)

Wilson, Robert, ex Linlithgow, sailor, d. 1698 in Darien,
    reg. 1708. (CC8.8.84)

Wilson, Robert, in Philadelphia, reg. 1873. (SC70.1.162)

Wilson, Robert, clergyman in Montreal, reg. 1881. (SC70.1.21)

Wilson, William, customs officer in Tobago, d. 25 Jan. 1831,
    reg. 1831. (SC70.1.44)(C480)

Wilson, William, ex Edinburgh, in Rockford, Illinois, reg.
    1885. (SC70.1.246)

Windram, Robert, ex Leith, mariner, d. 1698 in Darien, reg.
    1707. (CC8.8.83)

Winton, David, ex Edinburgh, mariner, d. 1699 in Darien,
    reg. 1707. (CC8.8.83)

Withards, Michael, ex Edinburgh, sailor, d. 1698 in Darien,
    reg. 1707. (CC8.8.83)

Wood, Edward, in St Kitts, d. 1824, reg. 19 Sep. 1825.
    (CC8.8.150)(SC70.1.33)

Wood, James Gardiner, in Zacaticas, Mexico, reg. 1899.
    (SC70.1.383)

Wood, Jane, in Clinton, Louisiana, d. 29 Oct. 1853, reg.
    1854. (SC70.1.85)(F1961)

Wood, William,merchant in Baltimore, Maryland, d. 1812,
    reg. 10 Apr. 1821. (CC8.8.147)

Wood, William, ex Galashiels, in Newberry, Luce C, Michigan,
    reg. 1899. (SC70.1.278)

Wooley, Charles Hitch, army officer in 16th Regiment of Foot,
    in St Vincent, reg. 21 June 1796. (CC8.8.130)

Wotherspoon, Elizabeth, in New York, d. 17 Jan. 1853,
    reg. 1857. (SC70.1.94)(H292)

Wright, David, merchant in Chicago, reg. 1888. (SC70.1.269)

Wright, Edwin, in Kentucky, reg. 1895.   (SC70.1.341)

Wright, Frances, in Cincinnati, USA, d. 13 Dec. 1852,
     reg. 1853.   (E3552)

Wright, James, ex Cariden, sailor, d. 1698 in Darien, reg.
     1707.   (CC8.8.83)

Wright, James, ex Paisley, seaman in America, d. Apr. 1859,
     reg. 1860.   (SC70.1.106)(H932)

Wright, John, ex Keith, sailor, d. 1698 in Darien, reg. 1733,
     (CC8.8.95)

Wright, John, ex Edinburgh,sailor, d. 1699 in Darien,
     reg. 1707.   (CC8.8.83)

Wright, John, in Clifton, Richmond Co, New York, reg. 1898.
     (SC70.1.371)

Wright, Nicola Eliza, in Jamaica, d. 20 May 1835, reg. 1858.
     (SC70.1.96)(H389)

Wright, Robert, ex Limekilns, carpenter in America, reg.
     11 Aug. 1829.   (CC8.8.152)(SC70.1.41)

Wright, William Lloyd, in Quebec, reg. 1896.   (SC70.1.352)

Wyllie, Alexander, ex Orkney, sailor, d. 1698 in Darien,
     reg. 1707.   (CC8.8.83)

Wyllie, William, schoolmaster in Tobago, d. 15 Aug. 1833,
     reg. 1854.   (SC70.1.82)(E3709)

Young, Alexander, in New Providence, reg. 1816. (SC70.1.14)

Young, Charles, ex Kippen, surgeon, d. 1698 in Darien,
     reg. 1707. (CC8.8.83)

Young, Elizabeth, in New York, d. 17 Jan. 1853, reg. 1857.
     (SC70.1.94)(H292)

Young, James, ex Abbotshall, mariner, d. 1698 in Darien,
     reg. 1707. (CC8.8.83)

Young, Jaet, ex Glasgow, in Montreal, reg. 1889. (SC70.1.285)

Young, John, officer in the Royal American Regiment, reg.
     31 Mar. 1766. (CC8.8.120)

Young, John, in Greensburg, USA, reg. 1869. (SC70.1.144)

Young, Patrick, ex Edinburgh, sailor, d. 1699 in Darien,
     reg. 1707. (CC8.8.83)

Young, Robert, in Nassau, Bahamas, reg. 1826. (SC70.1.35)

Young, Robert McLaren, in Patapoco River, USA, reg. 1890.
     (SC70.1.284)

Younger, James, ex Bo'ness, d. in America, reg. 1707.
     (CC8.8.83)

Younger, James, engineer in Philadelphia, reg. 1895.
     (SC70.1.342)